ACTING LESSONS FOR BEGINNERS

BY

SABAT BEATTO

DEDICATION

I want to express my gratitude to the students and teachers of P.S. 280 Q (Home of the Lionhearts), who assisted me in writing this book by providing feedback and suggestions at various points in the process.

To Dr. Dueño, Principal

A marathon is like life with its ups and downs, but once you have done it, you feel that you can do anything.

Table of Contents

PART ONE: BASIC ACTING 4
    HISTORICAL BACKGROUND OF ACTING 5
    ACTING: WHAT IS IT? 6
    TYPES OF ACTING 7
    PURPOSE OF ACTING 8
    WHO IS AN ACTOR? 15
    WHAT IS GENRE IN ACTING? 18
    BASICS OF ACTING 24
    NONVERBAL COMMUNICATION AN ACTOR MUST HAVE 28
    ACTING EXERCISES 37
    HOW TO PREPARE FOR ACTING 39

PART TWO: AUDITION 41
    WHAT IS THE PURPOSE OF AN AUDITION? 43
    HOW TO PREPARE FOR AUDITION FOR A PLAY 44
    HOW TO ANALYZE THE PLAY 48

PART THREE: FINAL REHEARSAL WITH COSTUME— PRESENTATION WITH AUDIENCE 55
    HOW TO GET THE AUDIENCE INVOLVED IN YOUR PRESENTATION 56
    CONCLUSION 64
    ASSESSMENTS 65
    GLOSSARY 72

Books by Sabat Beatto 76

PART ONE: BASIC ACTING

HISTORICAL BACKGROUND OF ACTING

550-220BC. the first known individual to ever perform on stage was a Greek guy named Thespis, and the earliest recorded instance of acting occurred in ancient Greece. He was born in the ancient city of Icarius, and he had a great deal of enthusiasm for the performing arts. Because most of his deeds were tragic, some people refer to him as the "founder of Tragedy." In addition to it, he acted in comedies and religious dramas.

Between 240 BC and 476 AD, the Roman government provided financial assistance for several forms of public entertainment, including theatrical art. Even further, the Roman government gave free entertainment over the whole Roman Empire to demonstrate to the people of Rome that their leader, Caesar, cared about them. Chariot races, gladiatorial contests, and theatrical performances were some forms of amusement that were popular with the Romans. There has been a significant shift in how acting has been conducted over time, and this shift is ongoing. How it operates, how it is shown, and how it is accessible have all been modified.

Before our current day, only members of society's upper class and nobility had access to theater talents. However, in today's society, anybody has the opportunity not only to observe but also take part in theatrical performances. Acting as a profession has seen significant transformations throughout the years as it has expanded beyond the confines of the stage and into film and television. There has been an evolution in the processes utilized by performers and directors.

ACTING: WHAT IS IT?

In a stage play, an episode of a television show, or one of the movies or flicks. The interpretation of a role or character is one definition of acting. Improvisation is another form of acting in which the actor comes up with a character on the spot and then acts out that character by making up lines and scenarios as they go along. An acting performance is judged to be successful when the actor successfully performs the role of the character they should in the manner in which the actor is expected to do so.

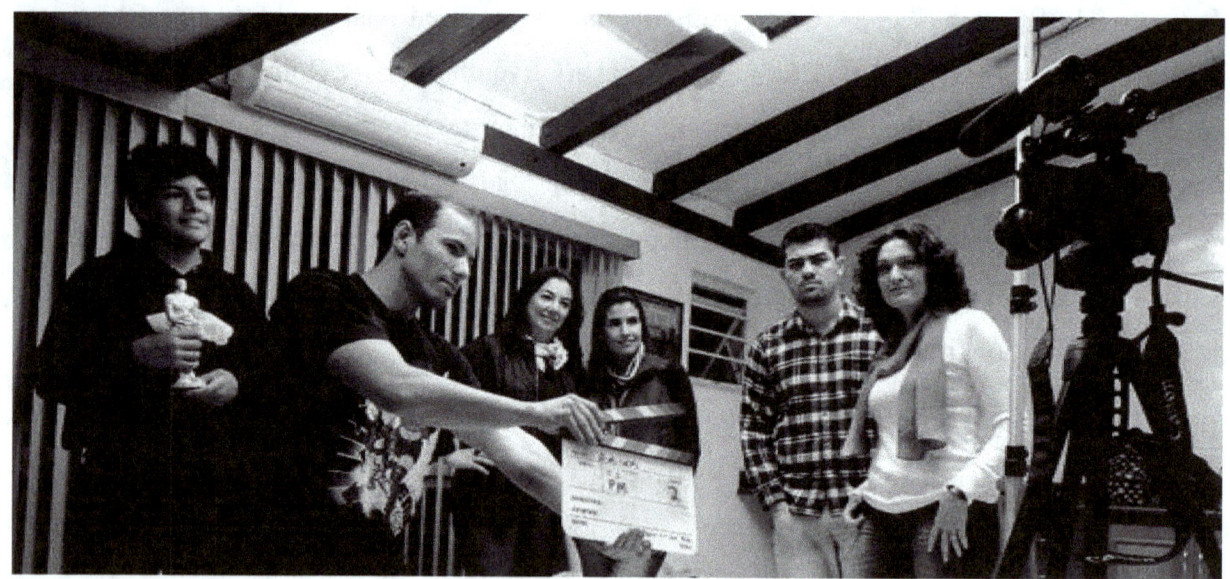

TYPES OF ACTING

➢ Classical Acting

Before the development of talking movies, actors gained experience and honed their craft by performing on stage in various forms of theater. And for the performers to conduct their play in such a way that the audience in the back row could see them, they had to be theatrical, exaggerated, and slow in their movements and talk very slowly and clearly.

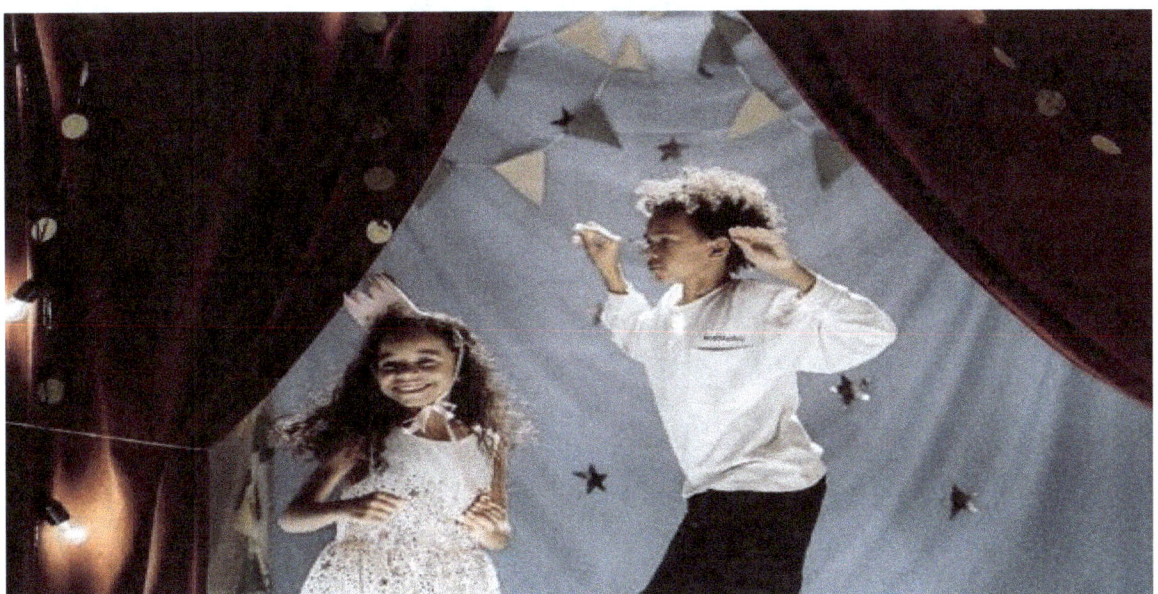

This "extremely dramatic" acting on stage began to lose popularity in the late 1920s when talking pictures (video) were introduced. This innovation, which eventually gave rise to what we now refer to as Classical Acting, was responsible for this shift.

> **Modern Acting**

The Moscow Art Theater is credited with being established by a Russian actor and director who is also credited with establishing modern acting. It is a form of acting that depicts genuine feelings drawn from the experiences someone has had in their own life.

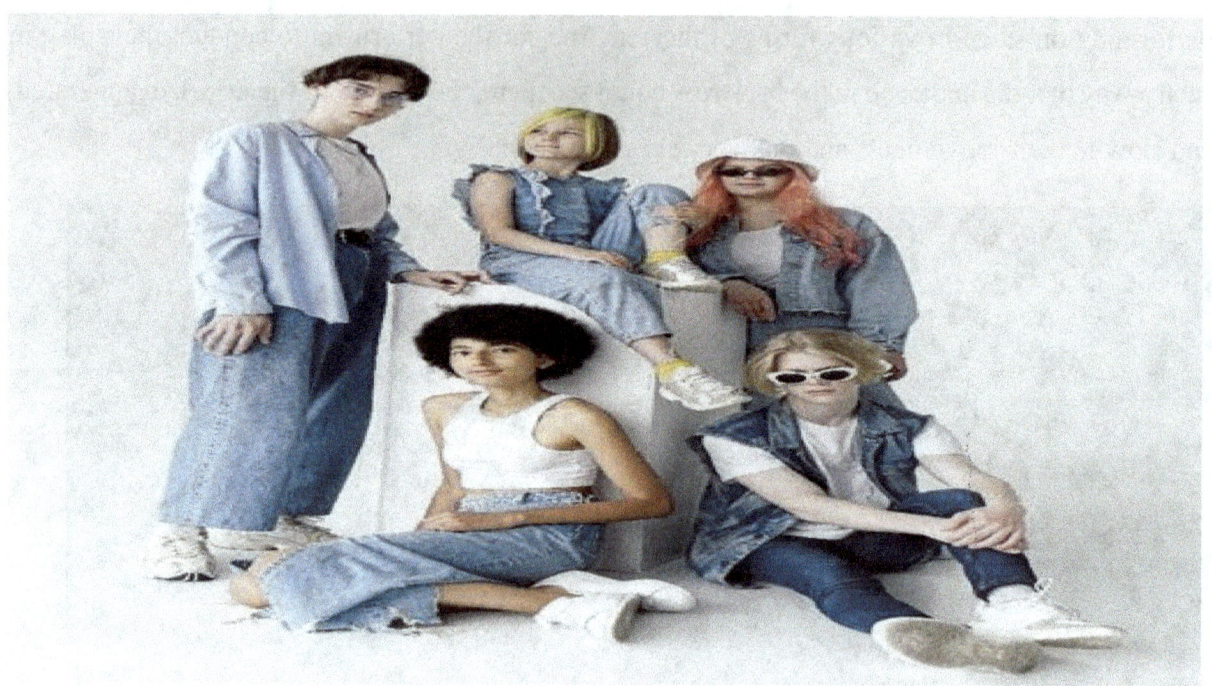

PURPOSE OF ACTING

Maintained a consistent level of. Even though some people are natural actors and were born with the talent to act, anyone who wants to be a good actor needs to practice and train their acting skills to become a good actor. Acting is a skill that needs to be developed, and some people are natural actors. Please take a moment with me as we discuss the significance of acting and the goals that it serves.

➢ Acting Allows Us to Transport Backward and Forward in Time

The process of acting is like operating a machine that may transport us to different points in the past. Actors can depict people in history who have had an impact on both our lives and our history. Actors can bring these types of stories to us by playing them out on stage in the same manner that history books teach us stories about individuals from the past who shaped our culture and history.

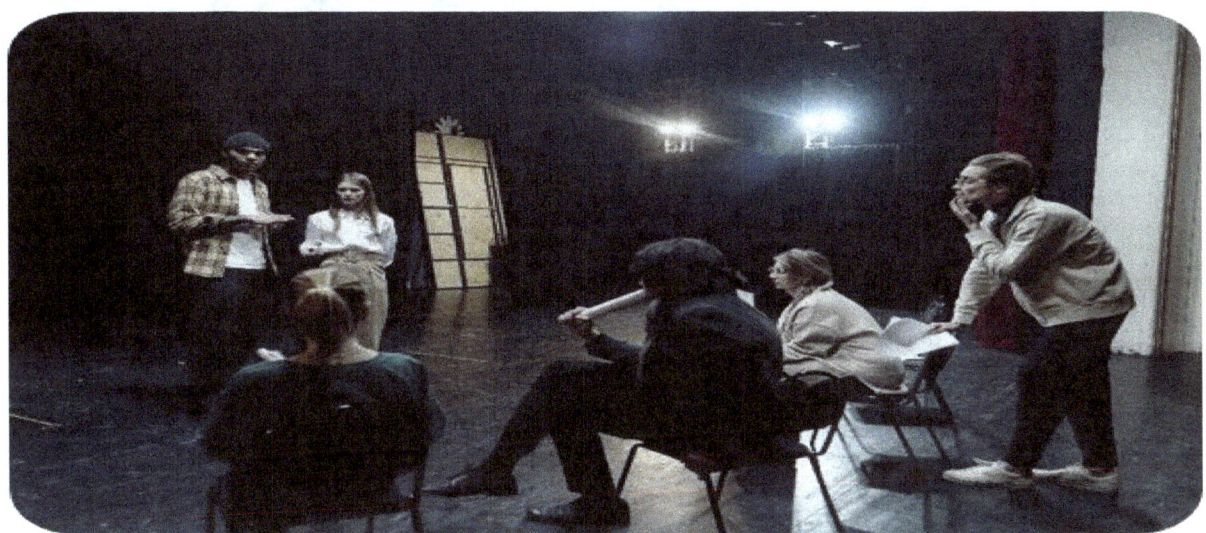

➢ Acting Provides a Window on Our Current Society

Because we are so preoccupied with our lives, we are frequently unaware of what is happening in society. However, via acting, we can gain a perspective on the events that are now taking place in our society. Actors have the ability, via their craft, to demonstrate how our society functions.

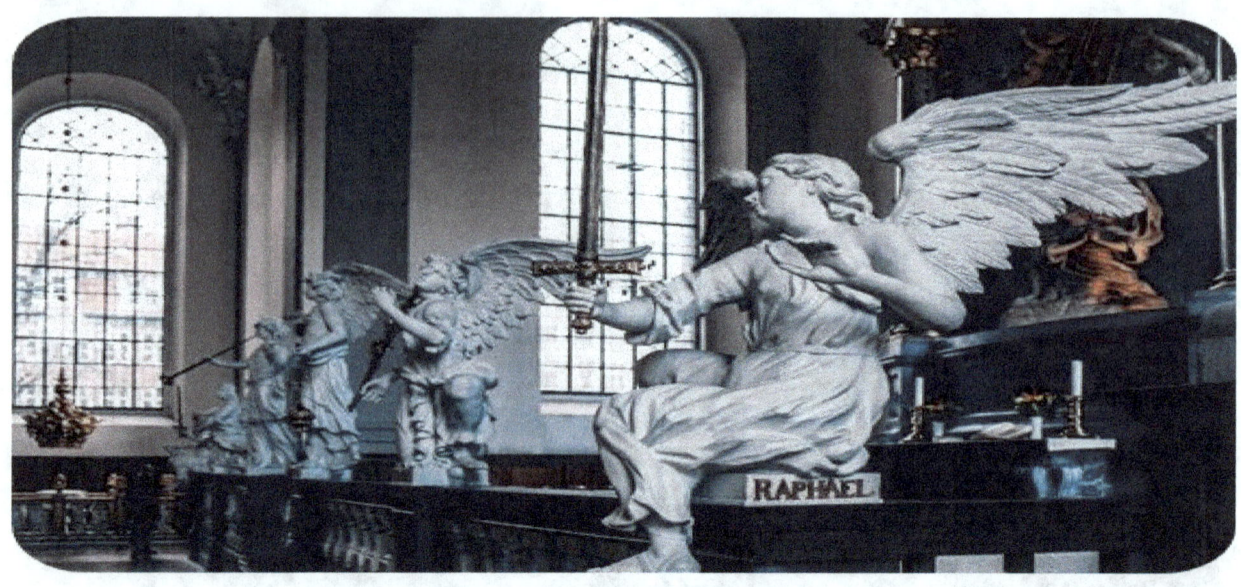

> **Acting Provides a Window on Our Humanity**

The truth about who we are as human beings may be discovered by doing. Actors have the ability to portray a wide range of human characteristics, including both positive and negative traits.

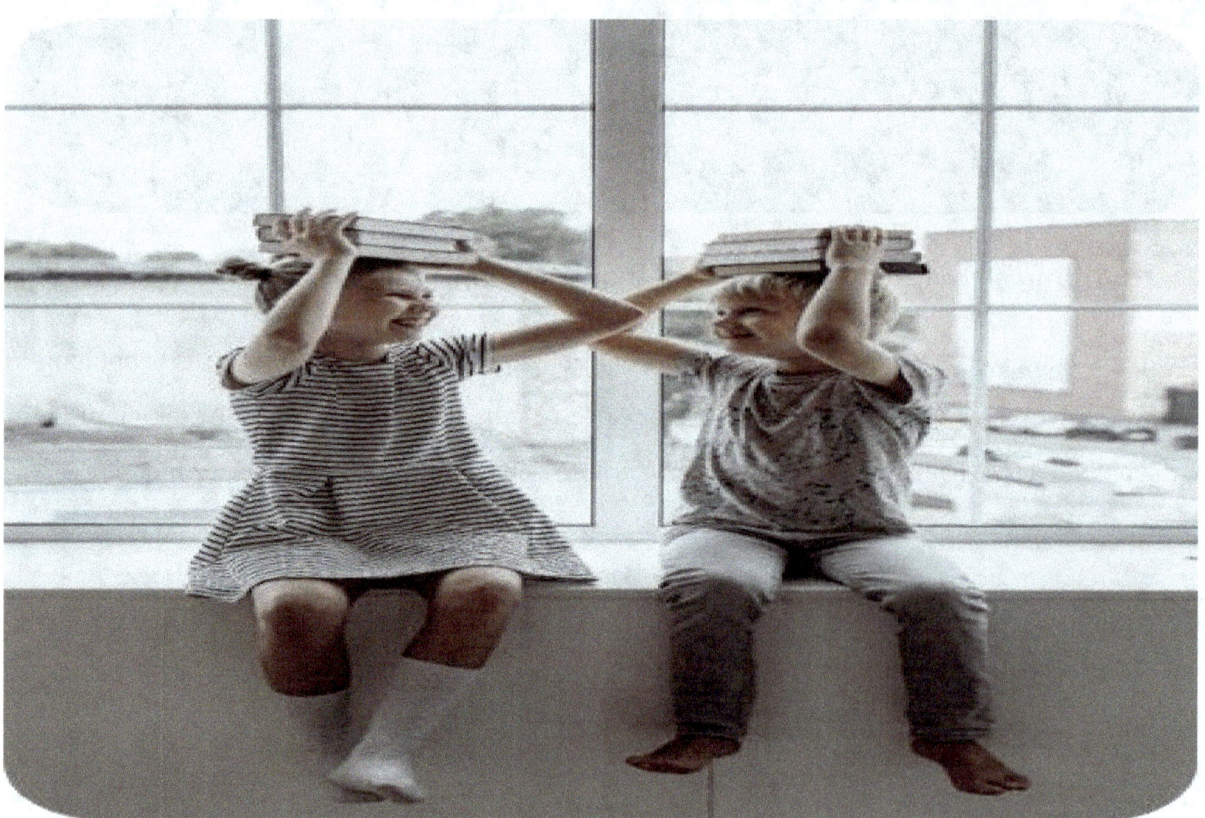

➤ Acting Opens Up the Opportunity for Important Discussions

People enter the realm of social communication when they engage in activities such as discussing the plot of a play. People can communicate with one another about the meaning of the performance they are acting in because acting allows them to do so.

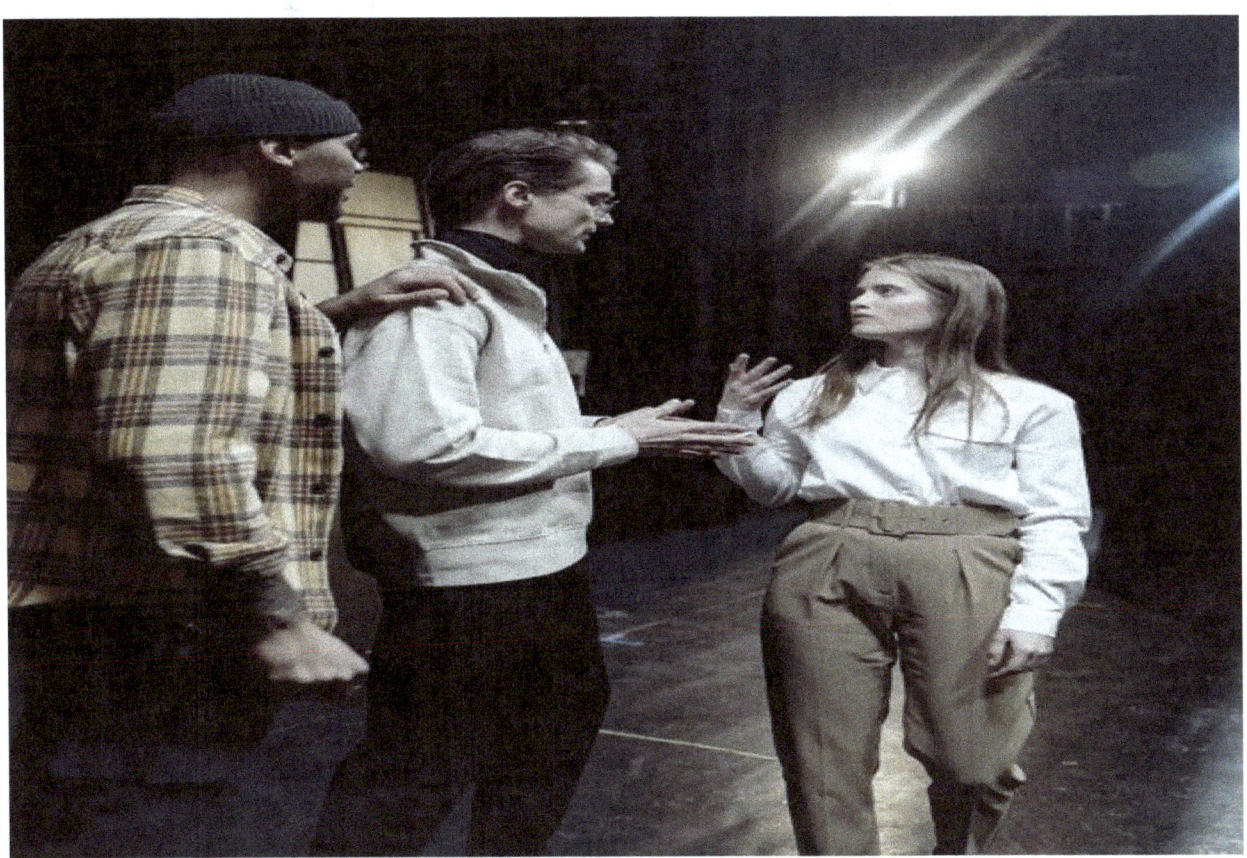

➤ Exploring other worlds and cultures is much easier when we perform in plays.

Individuals have the opportunity to portray people from various nations when they act on stage Therefore, acting enables us to become familiar with the traditions and customs of people who live in various parts of the world.

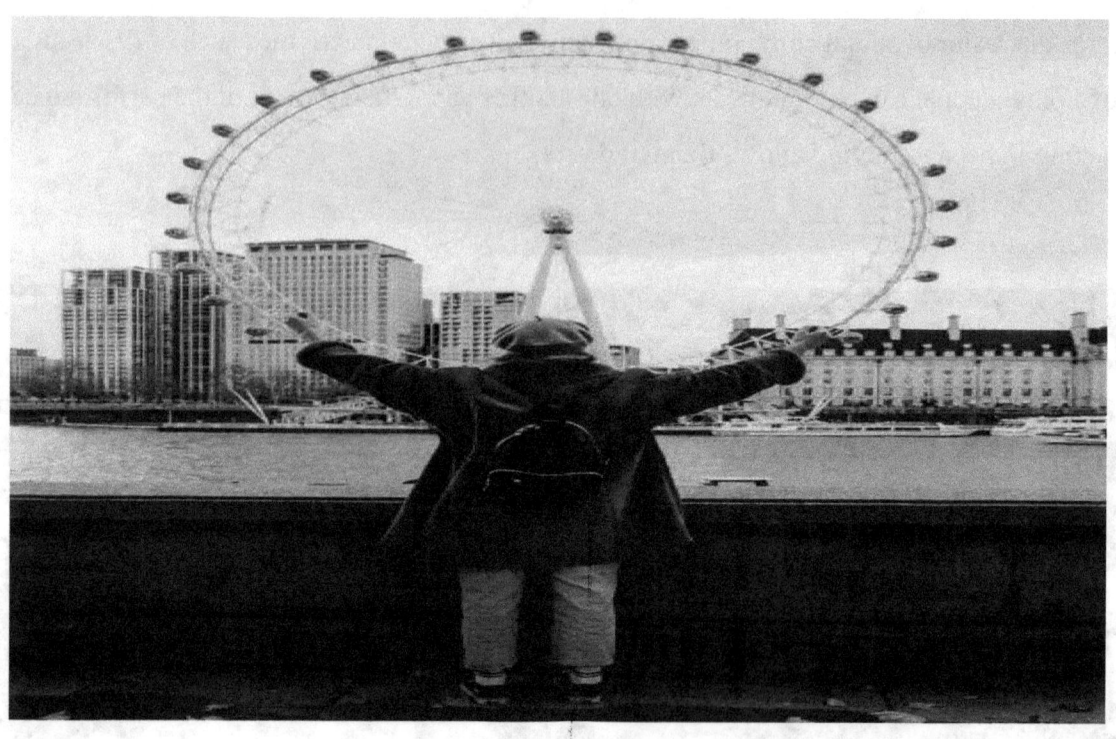

> **Acting Helps Us to Understand the Perspective of Others**

Through the art of acting, we have the opportunity to feel what it is like to live the life of another person. When an actor is asked to play someone else's role, they get the chance to experience firsthand what it's like to walk in those other person's shoes.

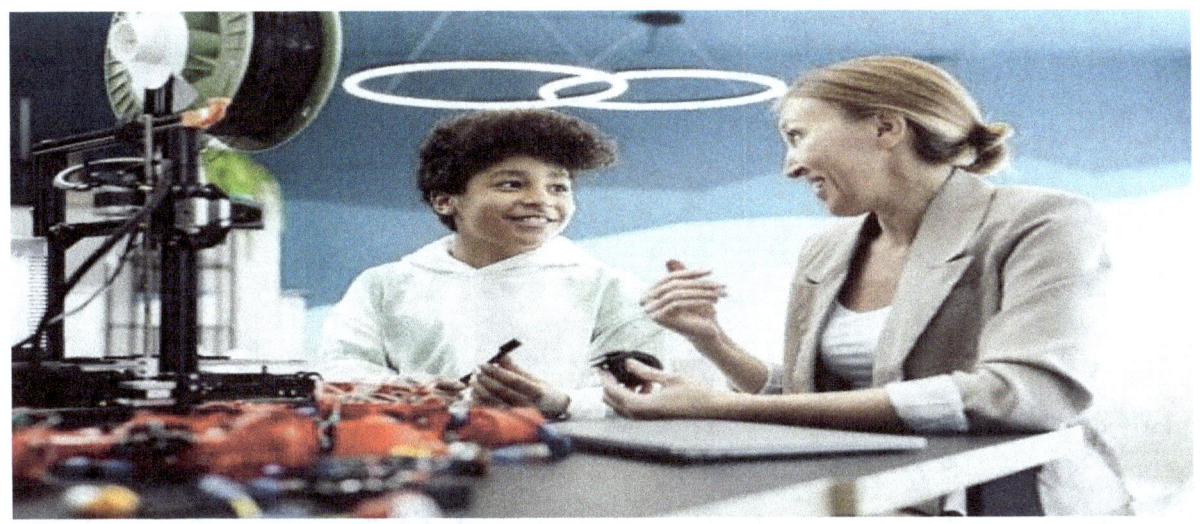

> **Acting Provides an Escape from Life's Challenges**

People are freed from the pressures, worries, and challenges they face during the day when they engage in acting because acting releases them from such things. When you are performing a role, regardless of how you feel, you are expected to take on the feeling of the character you are portraying to be taken seriously. If the audience expects your character to be joyful, you should also be happy. And by doing so, you are relieving yourself of the tension accumulated during the day.

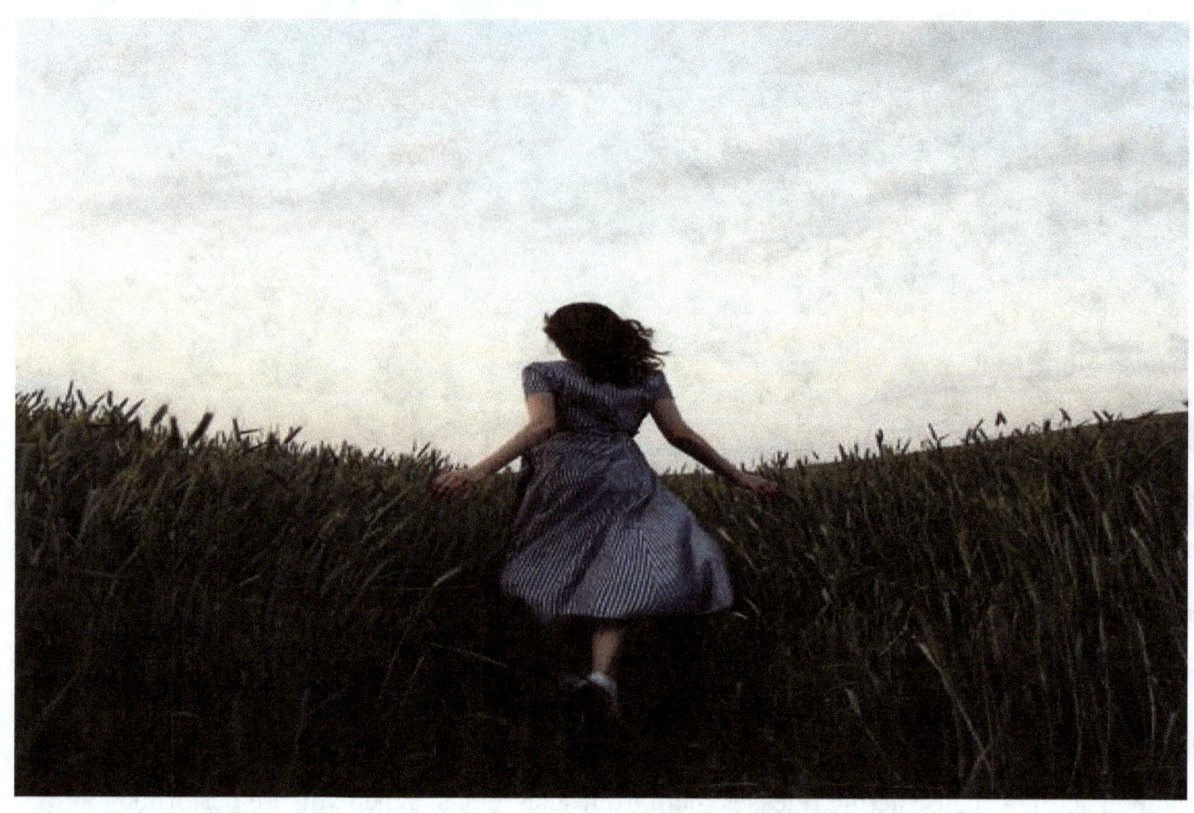

> **Acting Builds Confidence**

It takes a certain amount of bravery for an actor to be able to face an audience and perform a scene that involves intense emotion, such as a speech or a monologue. And as a consequence of that, acting may help you create confidence, which will assist you not just when you are acting but also in your day-to-day life. If there is an actor you are familiar with, you should look at them because you will find that they are brave individuals.

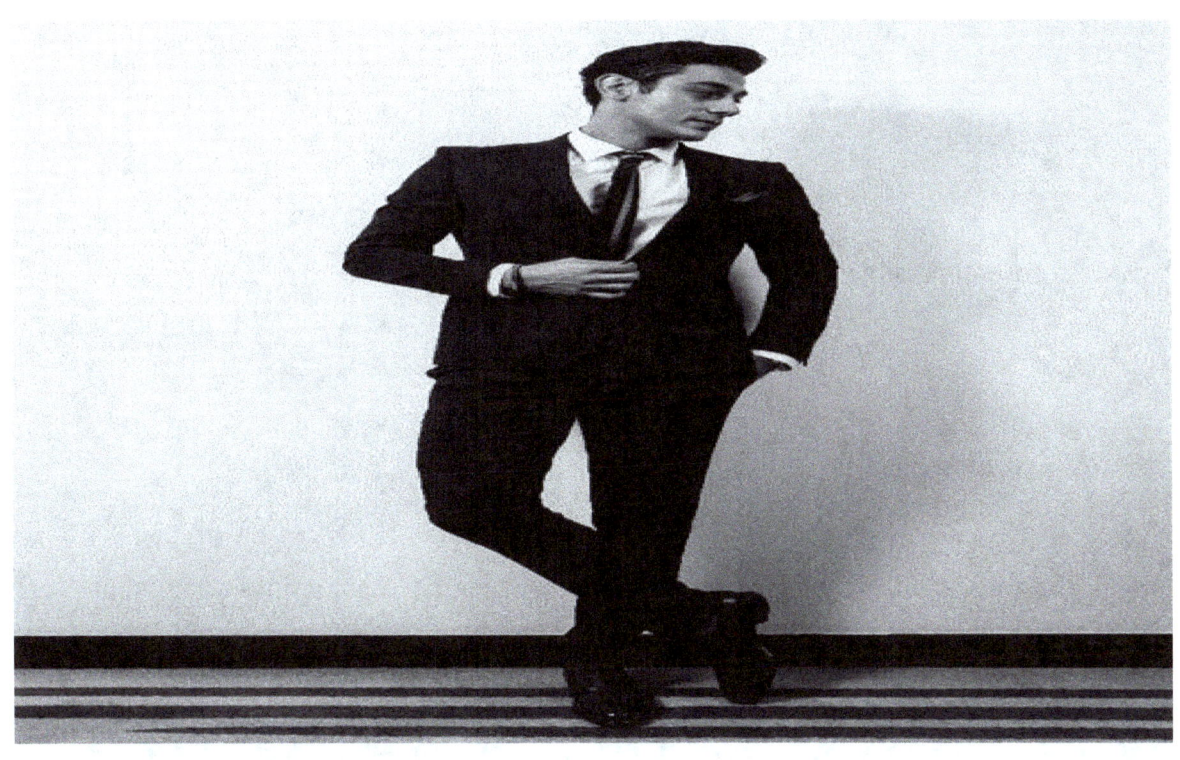

WHO IS AN ACTOR?

A person who acts in a movie or play is known as an actor, even though the term "actor" is often reserved for referring to men. Actors. However, some female actors who work in the industry want to be called "actors" rather than "actresses."

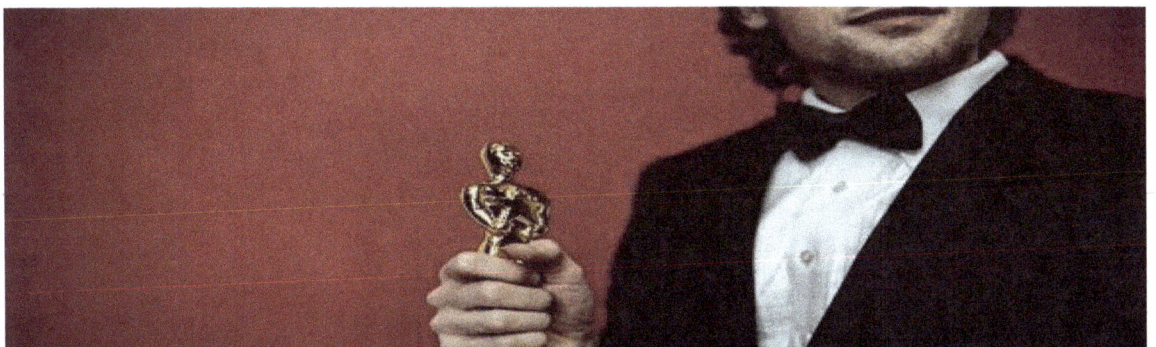

Let us look at several possible acting roles:

- ✓ **Star or Lead**

The principal actor in a play is known as the play's lead character. These groups of individuals are the ones who are highlighted in significant ways throughout the play.

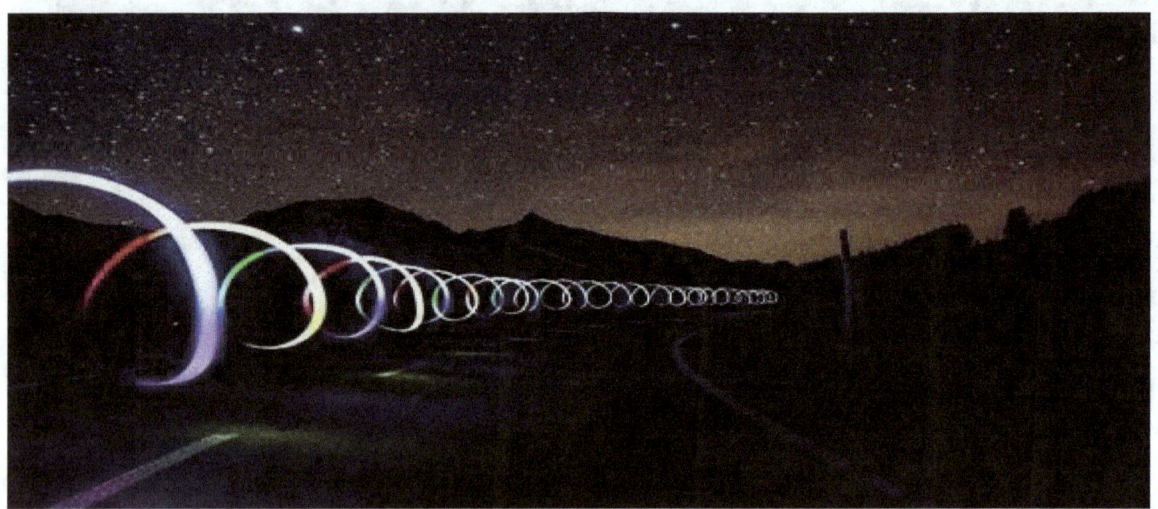

- ✓ **Supporting**

These are all of the players in a play who are required to speak at some point.

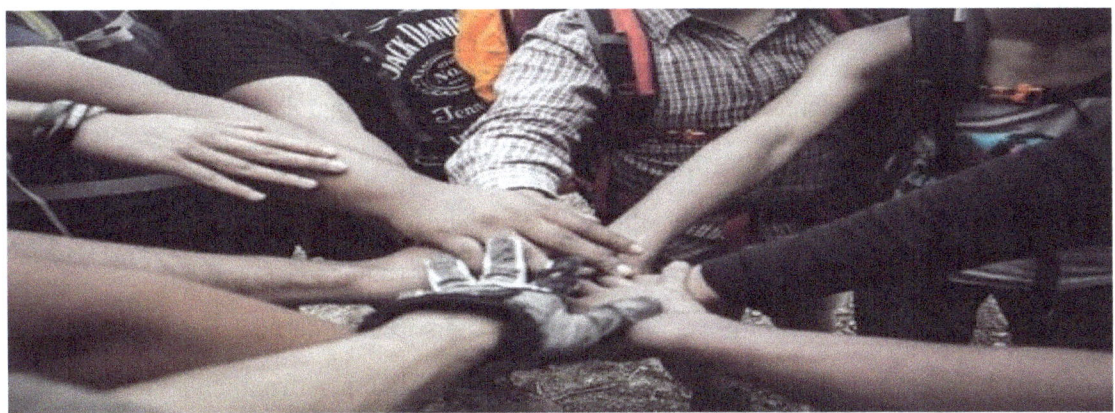

- ✓ **Extras & Backgrounds**

These are the individuals who are present but do not participate in the conversation by either speaking or doing anything other than standing or moving about in the background or front. They are only there to make up the necessary numbers for the play.

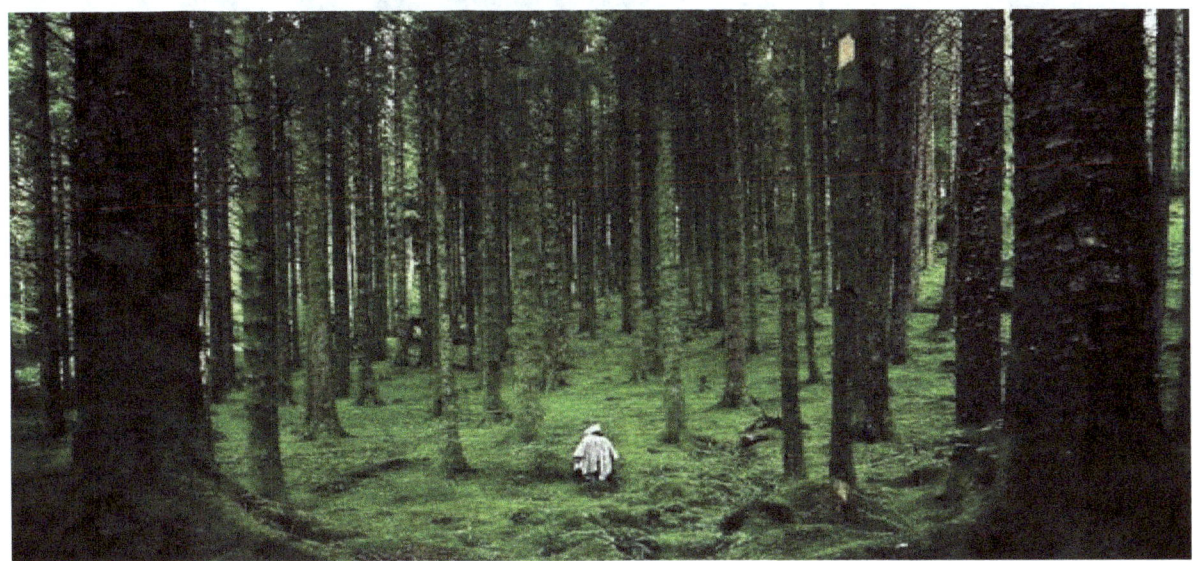

WHAT IS GENRE IN ACTING?

For those who want a more straightforward explanation, we may state that plays and acts are a part of certain genres. Being classified according to its genre When acts are broken down into their genres, the audience will have an easier time selecting the kind of show they want to see based on their personal preferences. A lot of people will only watch performances of a specific sort since they are the kind of genre they want to see. For instance, a person may decide to attend comedic plays exclusively because they find it to be the most entertaining live performance style.

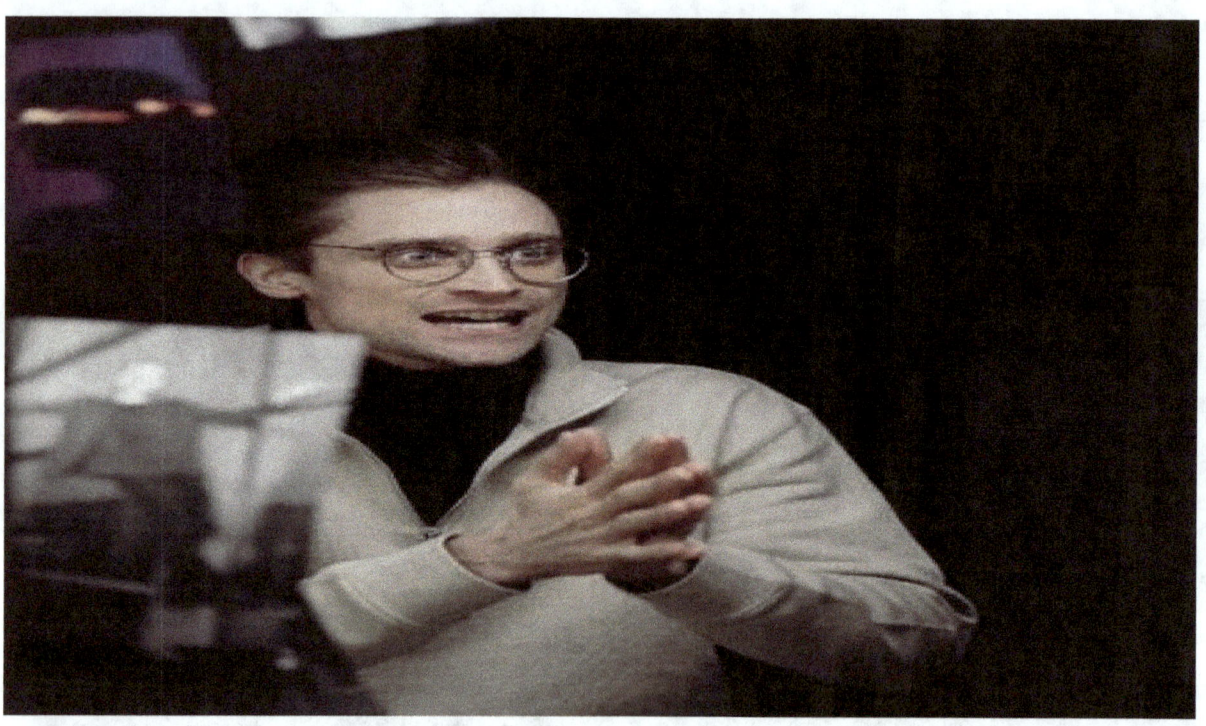

Below are the basic types of Genre available

- ✓ **Drama Genre**

A play, movie, or television program is considered to be dramatic if it conveys a story via action and dialogue, and that tale typically involves some sort of conflict or emotional turmoil.

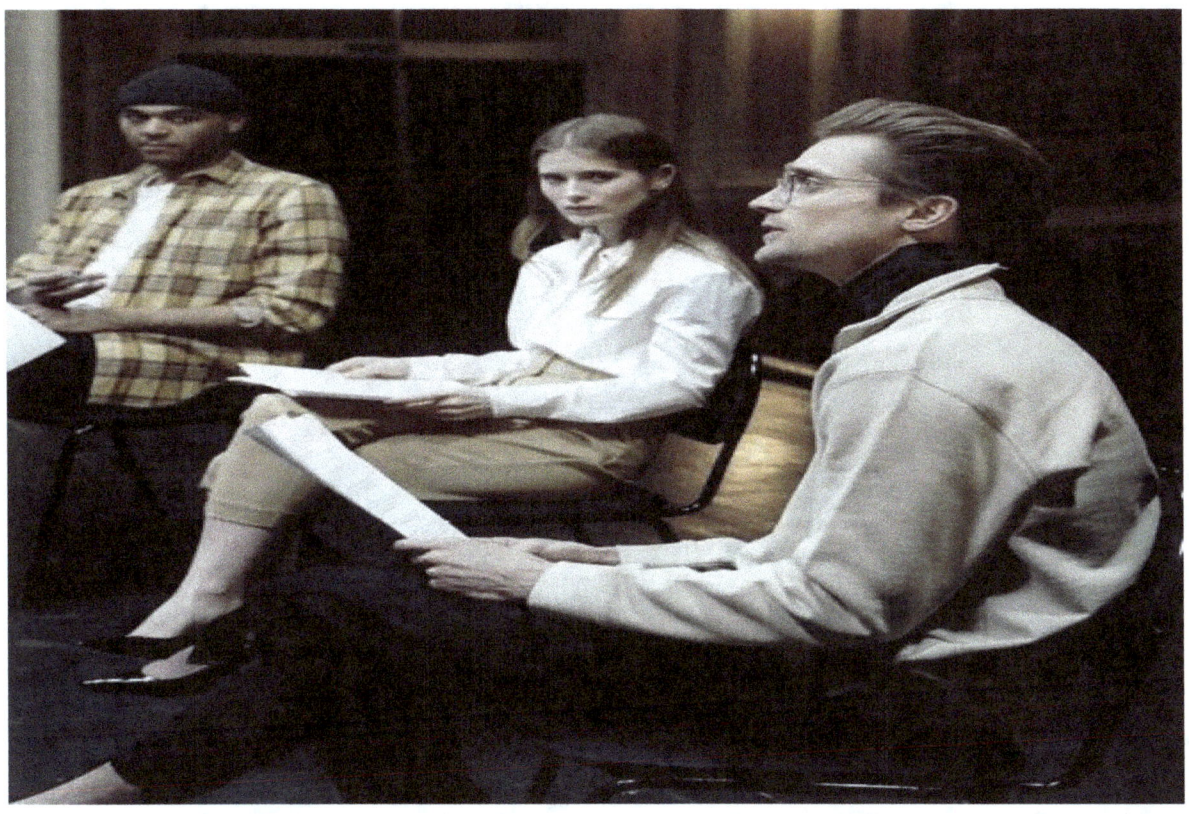

- ✓ **Comedy Genre**

A play, movie, or television program is considered to be comedic if its primary objective is to elicit laughter from its audience.

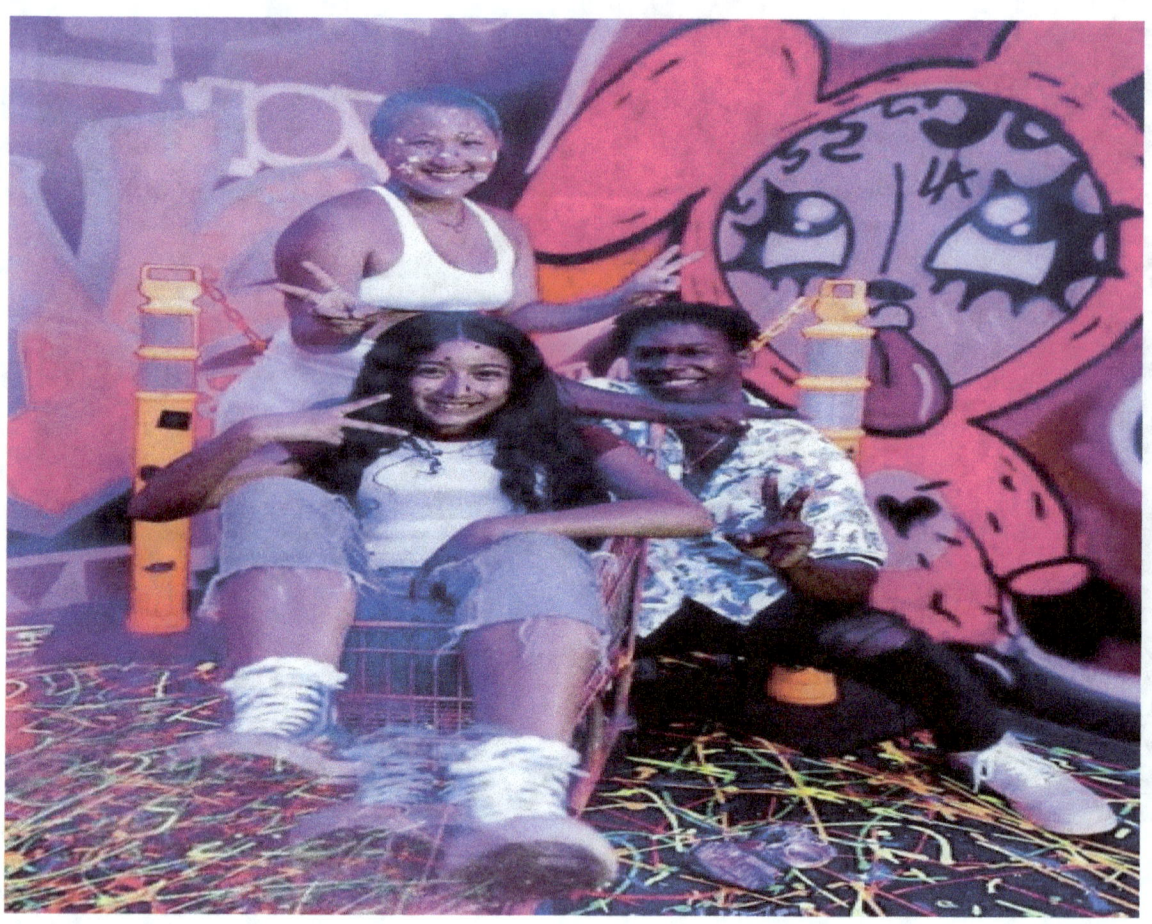

Romance Genre

Romance plays are essentially love stories that focus on the development of a romantic relationship between two characters throughout the course of the play's plot.

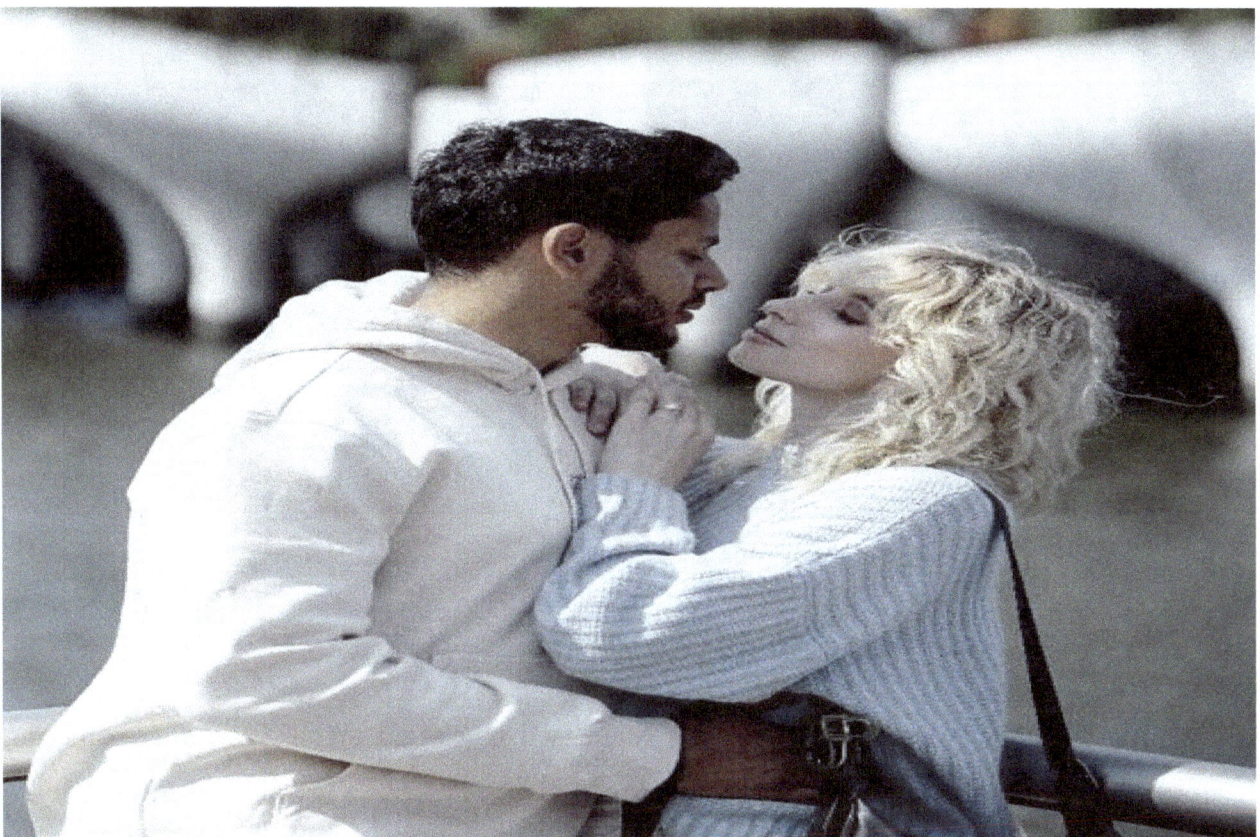

The term "rom-com" refers to a romantic comedy that also has elements of humor (Romantic Comedy).

✓ **Adventure Genre**

The game of adventure is fraught with peril and challenges, and the journey itself is fascinating and memorable due to the challenges and perils encountered.

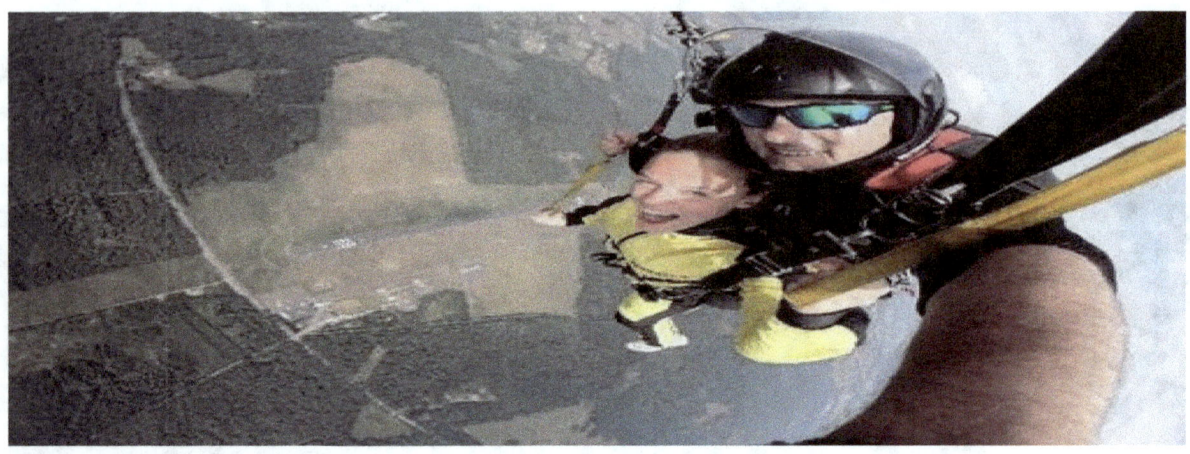

✓ **Play Genre**

A piece of dramatic writing known as a play is intended to be acted out on stage rather than being read out loud to an audience. Playwright is the term used to describe a person who creates plays.

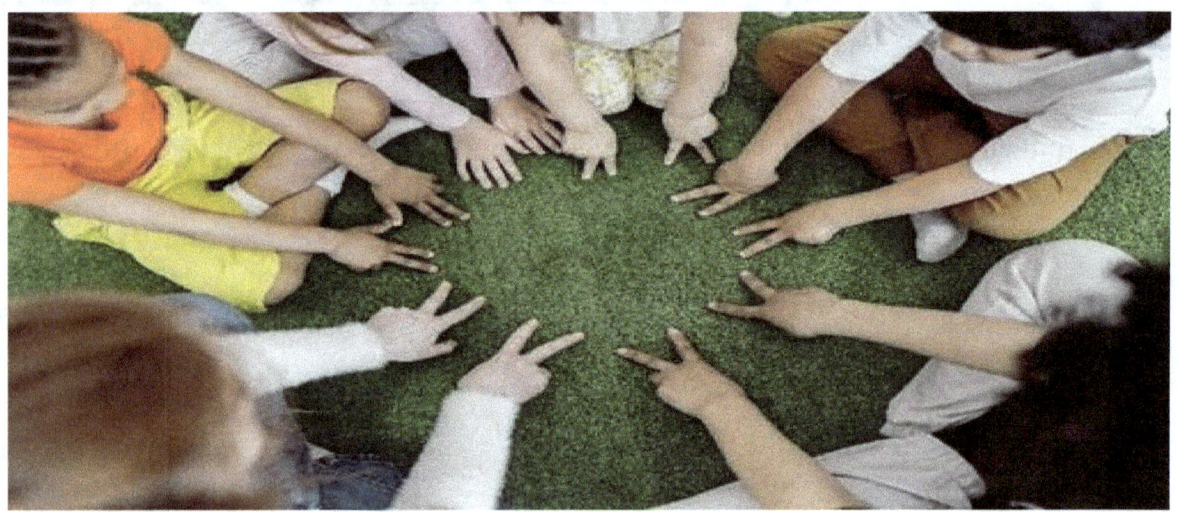

✓ **Fantasy Genre**

This is a style of play that takes place in the mind rather than in the real world and is generated by imagination.

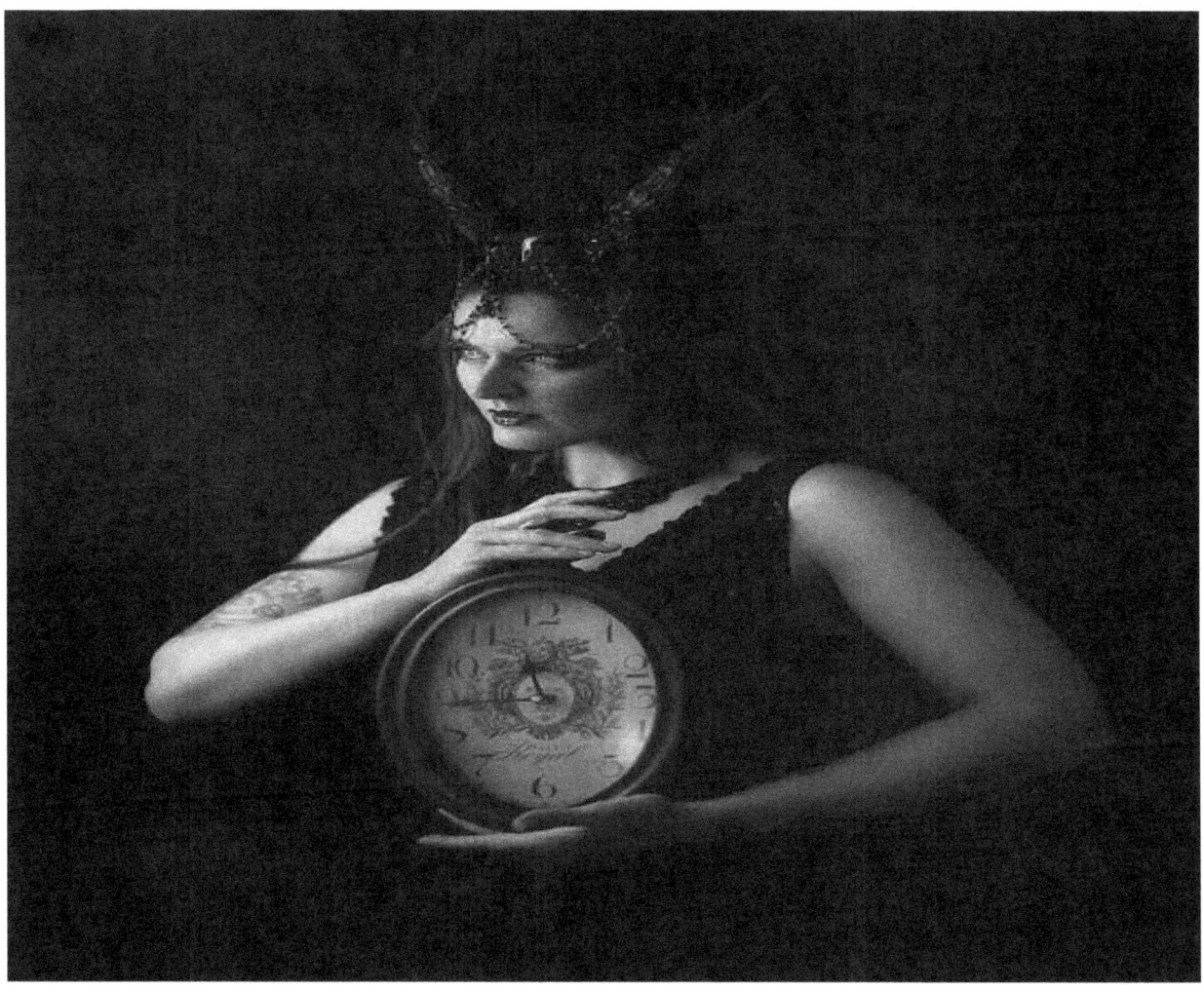

BASICS OF ACTING

Carry it out without making any errors whatsoever. On the other hand, regardless of how well an actor prepares for a performance, there is a good chance that once they take the stage, they will not perform as well as they did in rehearsal. It's possible that neglecting some fundamental acting norms was the root of the problem with the execution in some cases.

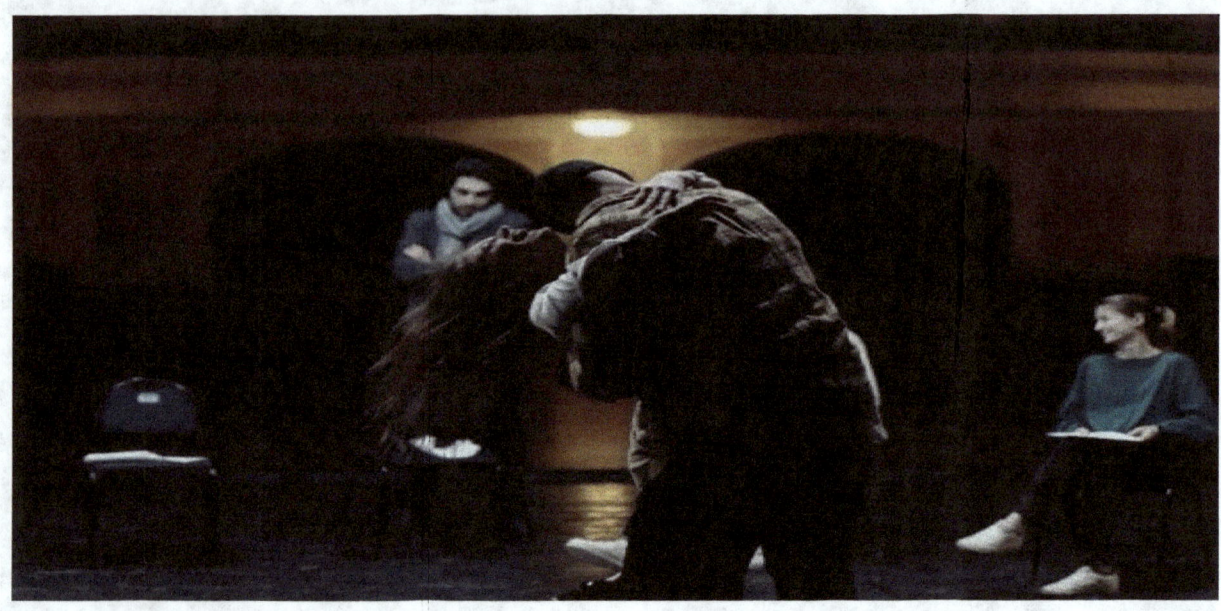

The following is a list of the most fundamental things to keep in mind before going onstage to perform.

❖ **Where are you?**

Take a minute before you begin the performance to think about where you are mentally and give yourself some time to do this. You have to link your presence and your consciousness to the location you are in right now.

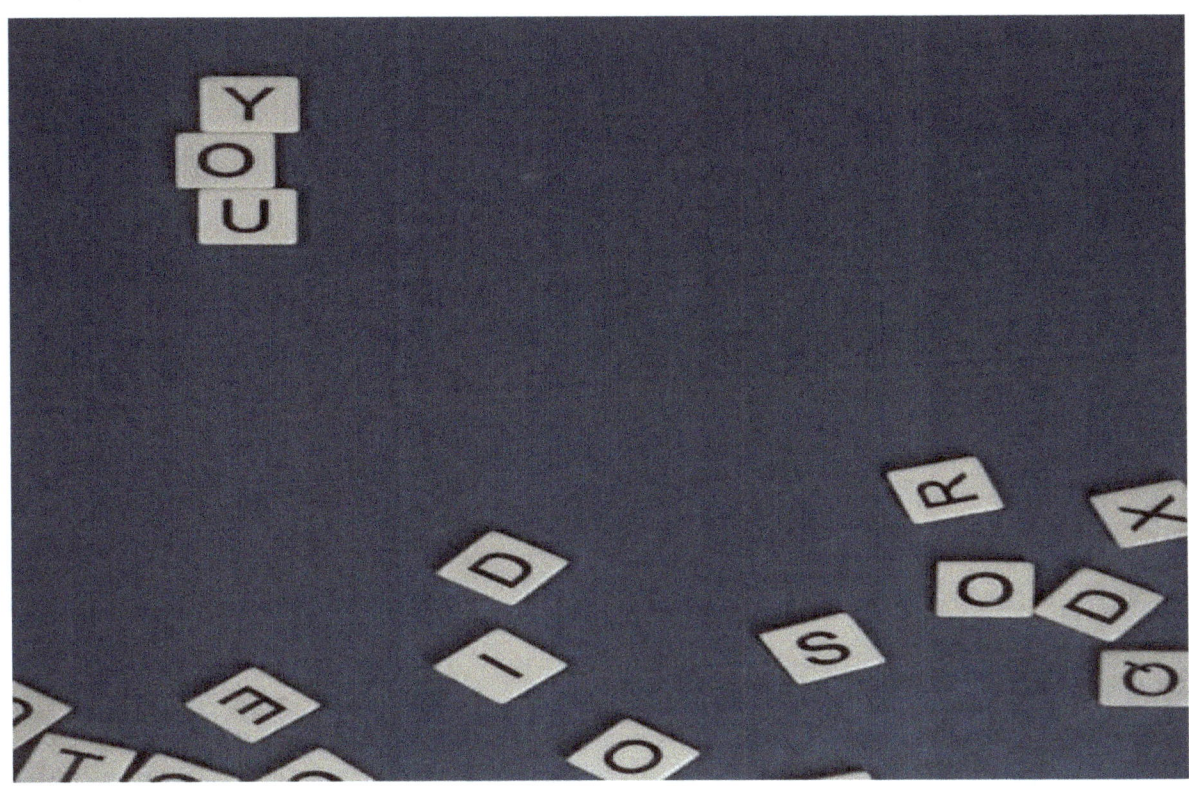

What is your relationship?

As an actor, you need to have a firm grasp of the audience you are playing for and the significance they hold for you. If you value their opinion, then you should provide your best effort to win it.

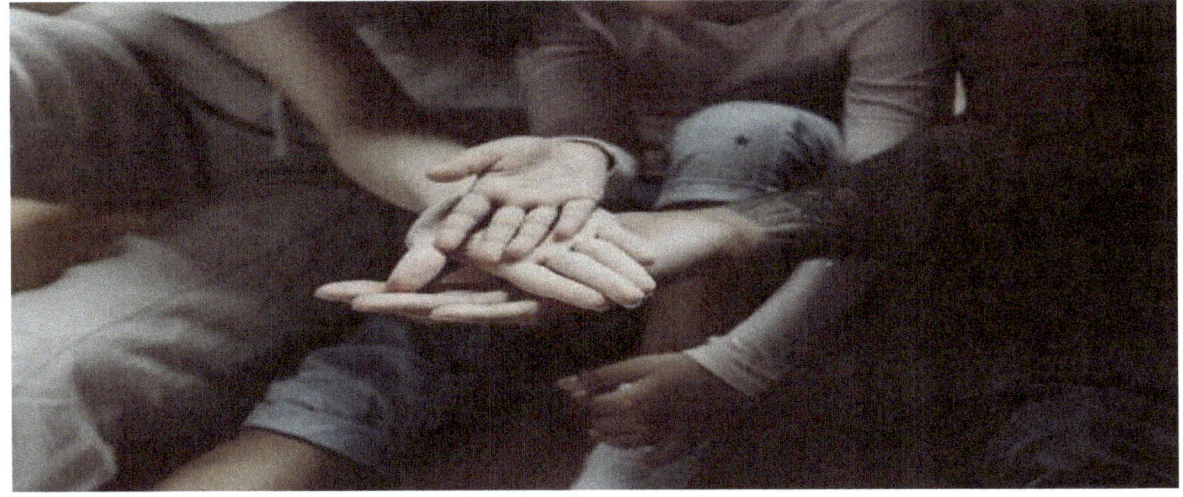

- ❖ **What is happening?**

Your performance ought to be understandable in terms of the information it tries to convey.

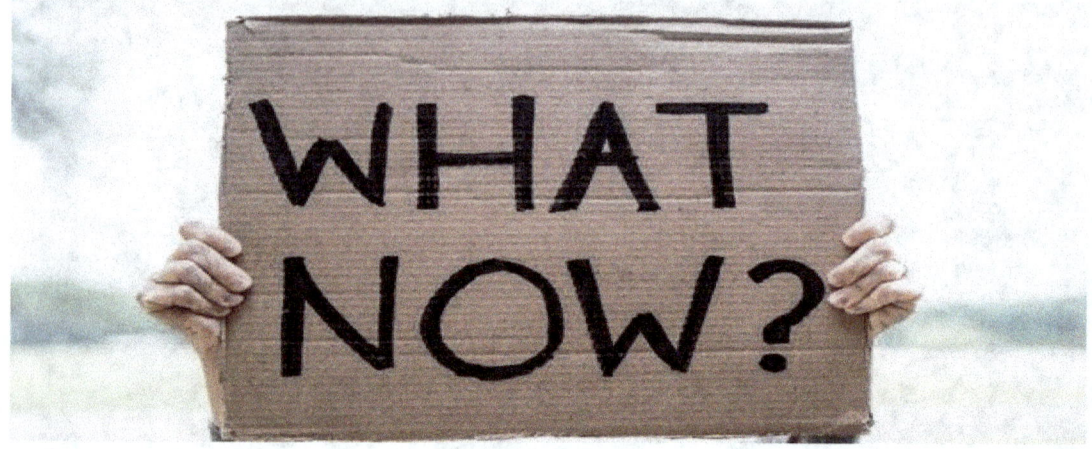

Your performance should have a primary message that it is aiming to convey to the audience, and you must keep that message in mind throughout the entirety of the performance. This is analogous to the top article that appears in a newspaper.

- ❖ **What are you doing?**

As an actor, you are portraying a character, which is expected to fulfill a certain function in the story. You have to make sure that this job can be achieved, and it has to be supportive of the message you want to convey to others. Therefore, you ought to be conscious of what you are doing.

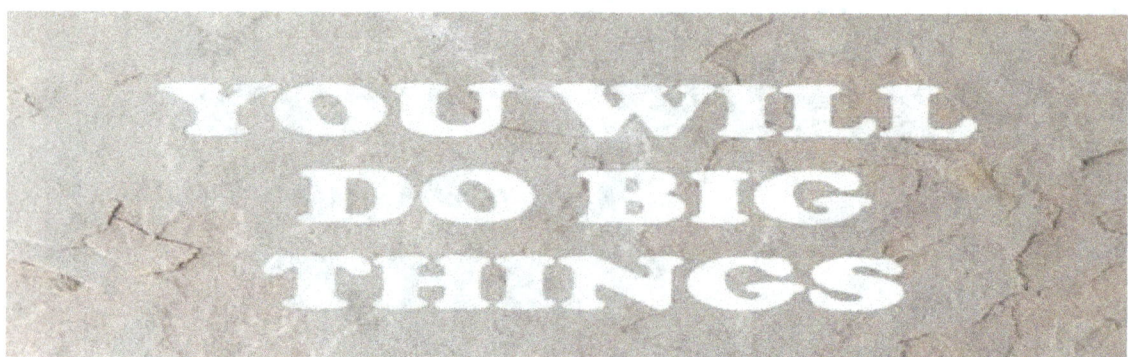

Never lose sight of the fact that you have to let the performance carry you. Suppose your character is expected to cry at a given moment in the performance. In that case, you should let the emotion associated with that particular scene take control of you so that you may successfully portray the character's tears. Do not keep anything back in any way. Let the scene take control of you.

You could feel anxious when you look out at the crowd or while you're on stage, but you need to pull your thoughts away from such things and concentrate on the part you're intended to play. And if you have done a good job practicing and rehearsing, it shouldn't be too difficult for you to get into character and deliver an outstanding performance.

NONVERBAL COMMUNICATION AN ACTOR MUST HAVE

People are able to understand us based just on the expressions on our faces. The majority of communication between humans consists of nonverbal cues. Our facial expressions, hand motions, and overall body language are all examples. You need to be able to learn how to utilize your body more in order to communicate with the audience, especially if you are only required to act and not talk much during the performance.

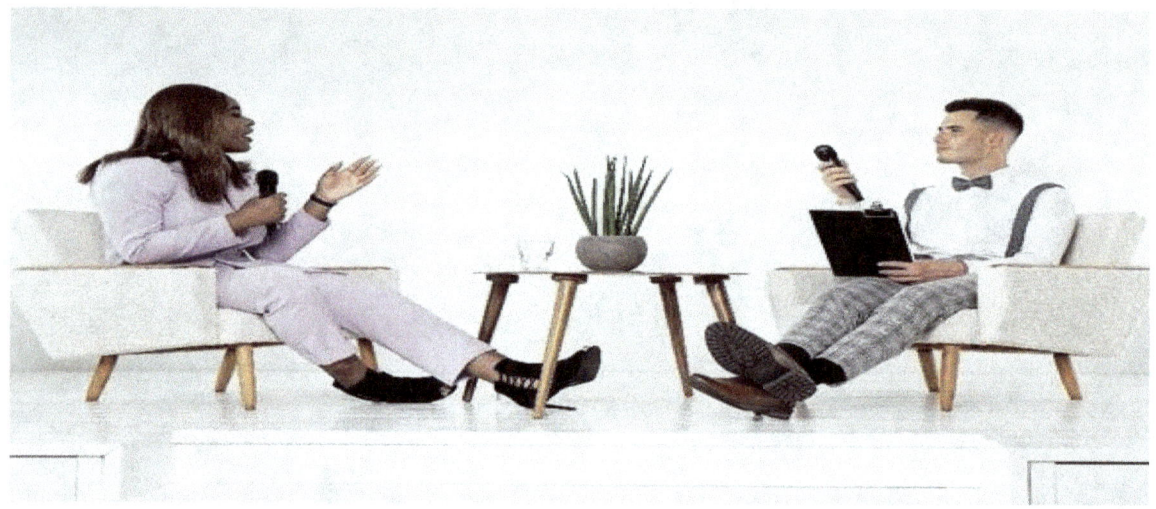

In the following paragraphs, I will outline eight nonverbal communications and behaviors that you may use in your performance.

- ✓ **Your face**

The expressions we produce with our faces are responsible for the vast majority of the nonverbal communication we convey to others. You should also be aware that you need to obtain the appropriate facial expression to be able to communicate with the people in your audience but rather will confuse them. Your audience can tell what emotion you are experiencing just by looking at your face, whether it be fear, happiness, perplexity, surprise, anger, grief, disgust, or disdain.

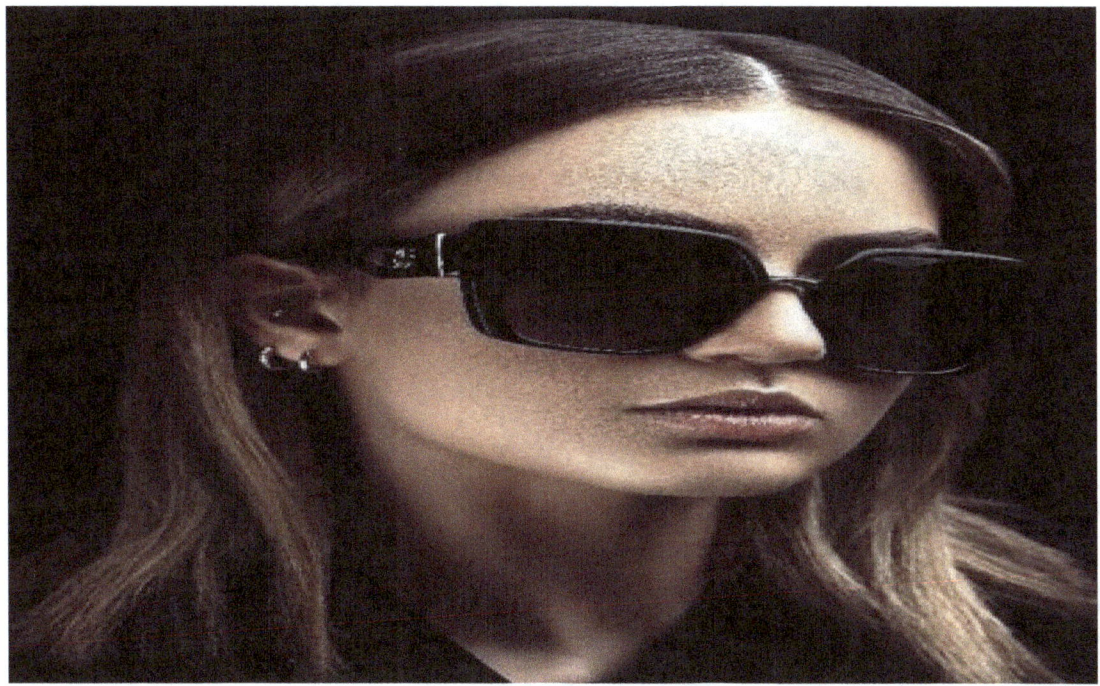

- ✓ **Your hands**

Your audience will be able to understand what you are trying to say more clearly if you make movements with your hands. You may communicate with your audience more effectively by hand gestures, such as counting out loud with your fingers. You can get your audience's attention on anything by pointing it out, and you can say farewell to them by just waving your hand. Neither of these actions requires the use of any words.

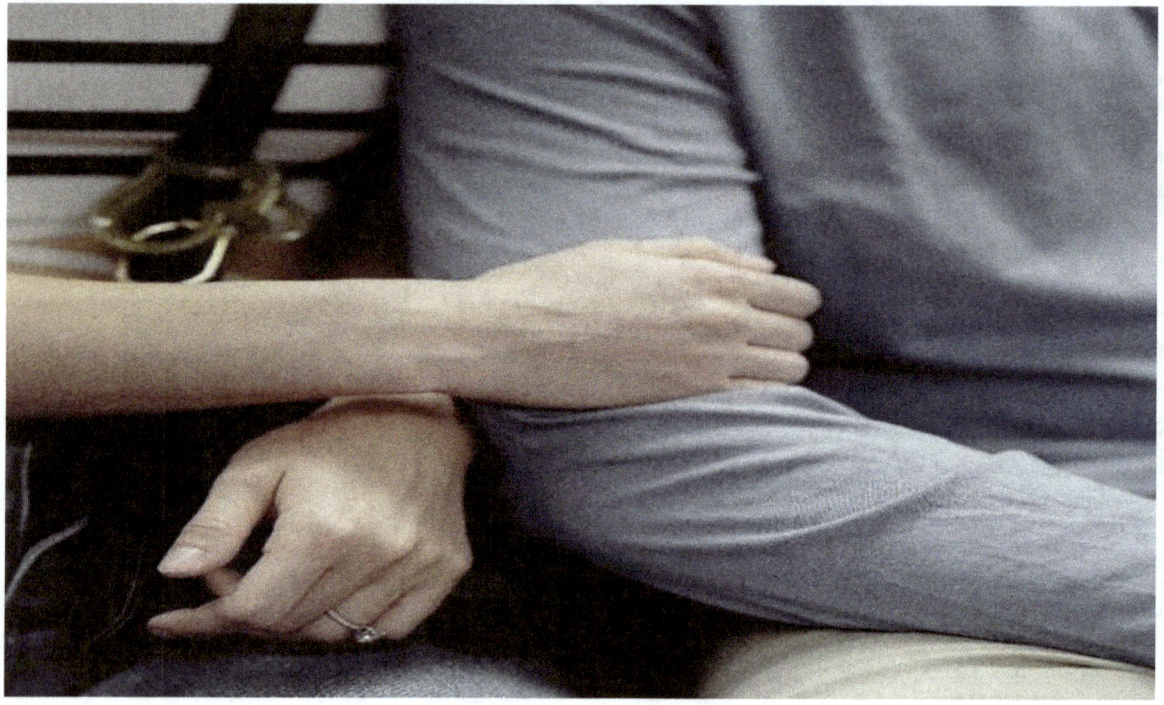

- ✓ **Your voice**

The meaning of a statement can be altered simply by changing the pitch at which it is spoken. Words can have different connotations depending on how they are said and how loudly they are spoken. If you say the same thing with a weak tone, you might not be able to capture your audience's attention, but if you say the same thing with a powerful vocal tone, you can get your audience's attention.

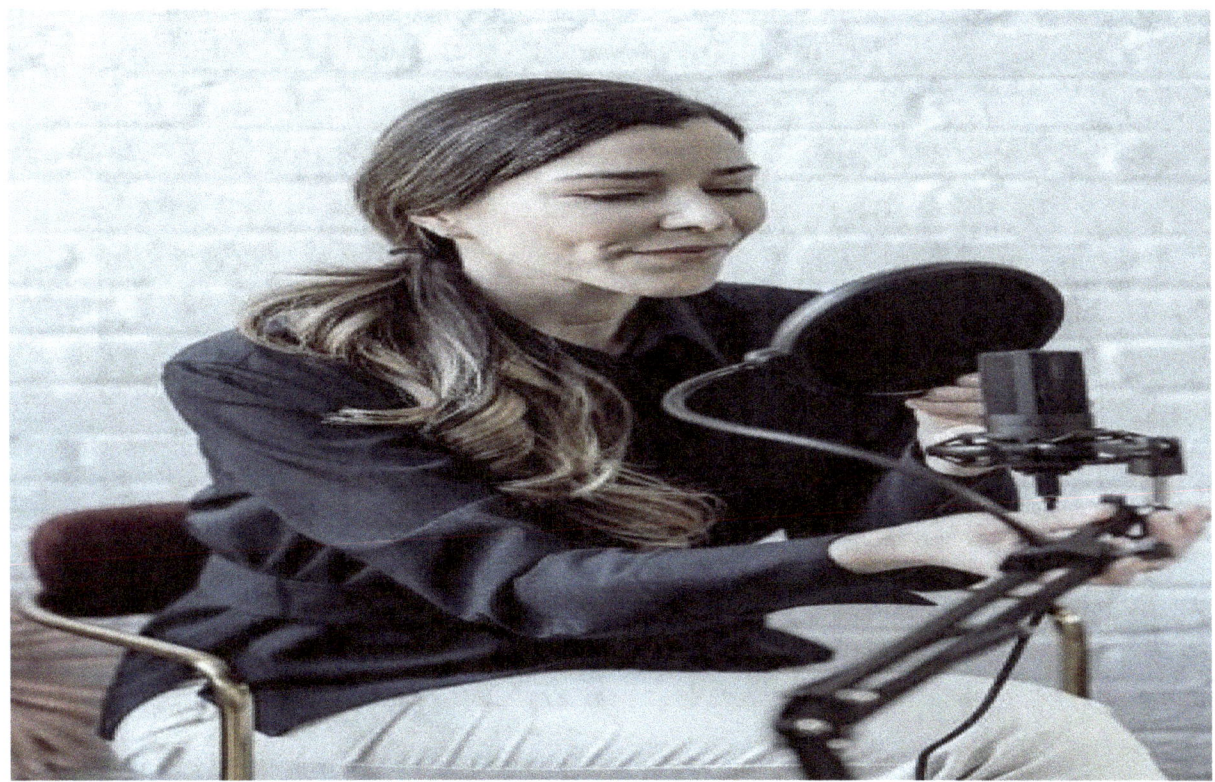

- **Your body**

You don't have to rely just on your facial expression to convey the range of feelings you're experiencing; your body language may do the trick just as well. When we make a hasty retreat from something, it may be a sign that we are afraid of that item. Therefore, it is evidence of dread. Another sign that we are perplexed is if we find ourselves scratching our heads frequently. When we yawn, it might mean that we are hungry, tired, or other things.

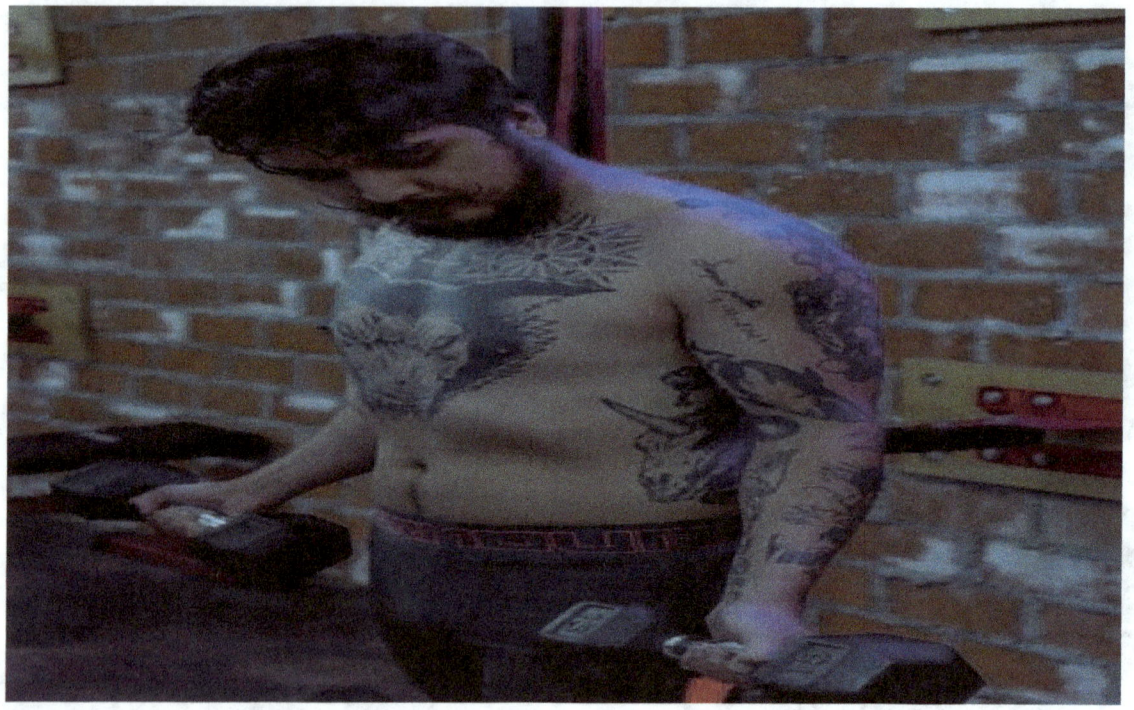

- ✓ **Personal space**

Proxemics is the study of the relationship between the amount of space we believe we require and the distance we require. Various factors influence how much space we require, and each of these might convey a certain message to the people who are watching. For instance, being close to someone or something might signify intimacy, while being far away from something can signify repulsion.

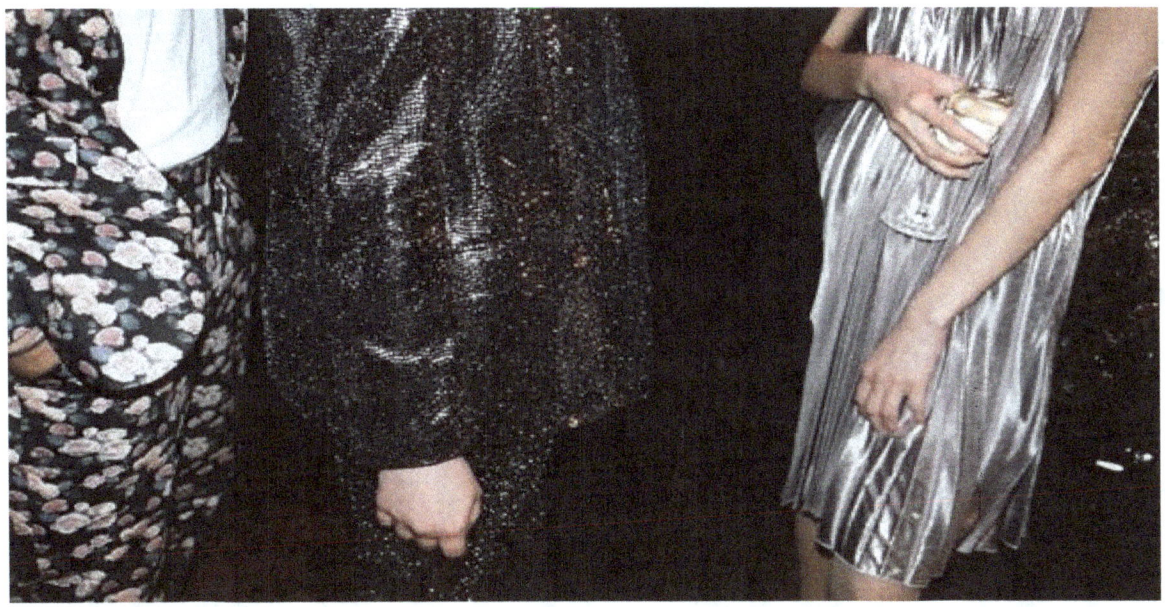

- ✓ **Your eyes**

The term "eye gaze," also goes by the names gazing, staring, and blinking, is another term for a nonverbal indication with a great deal of weight. In addition, they may be utilized to convey a specific message to the audience you are addressing. We have a habit of blinking more quickly, and our pupils dilate when we encounter persons or things that we find enjoyable. On the other side, when we are furious, our eyes are less likely to blink, and we tend to fixate our focus on something. When we blink frequently, it may signify that we are unprepared, disengaged, or experiencing great anxiety. When we glance around an excessive amount, it may indicate that we are afraid or anticipating something to happen.

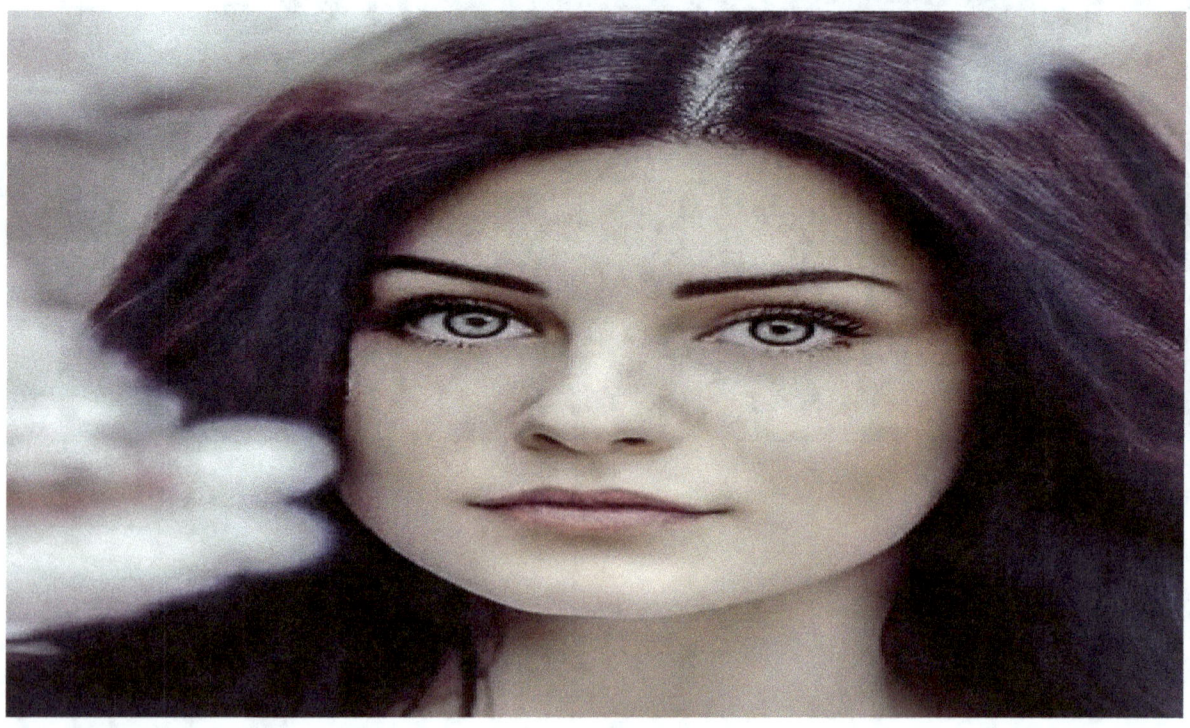

- ✓ **Your touch**

Haptics is the name given to a mode of communication that is founded on the sense of touch. It is another nonverbal behavioral indicator that should be taken into consideration. Your touch has the power to communicate a wide range of feelings and emotions, including affection, familiarity, sympathy, desire, and many others.

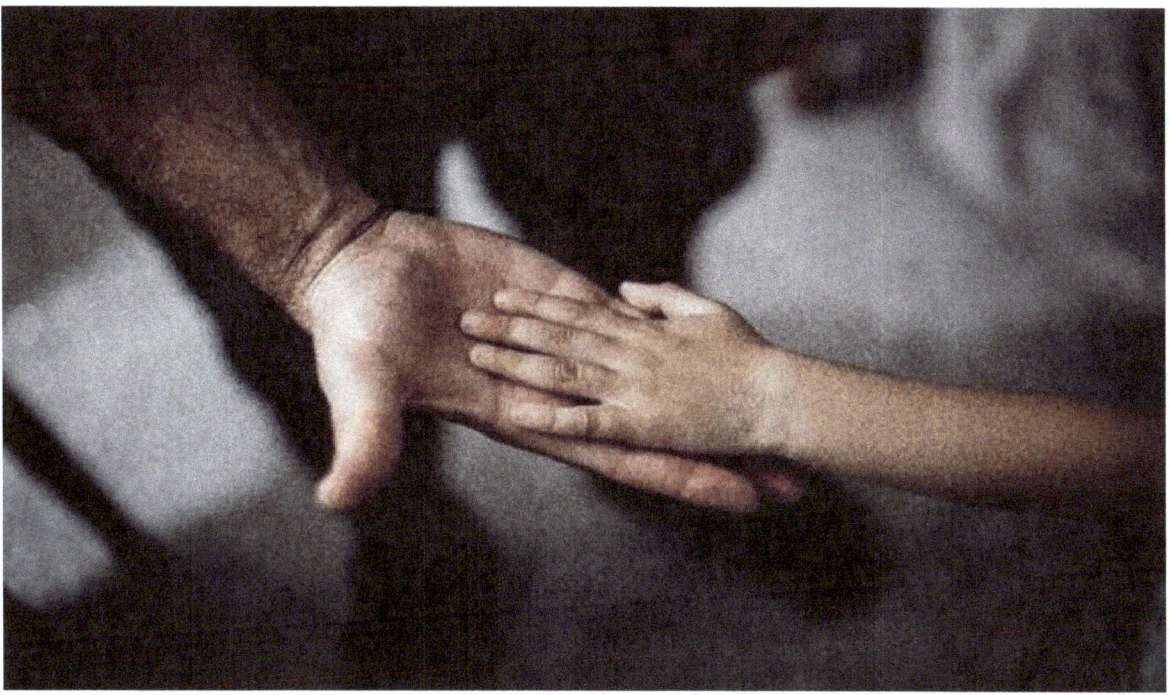

- ✓ **Your looks**

In order to effectively communicate with your audience, the selection of the dress, hairdo, and cosmetics you wear, along with any other factors that determine how you seem, is very crucial. When you consider the snap judgments you make about other people based on their outward look, you may begin to appreciate the significance of appearance in communication.

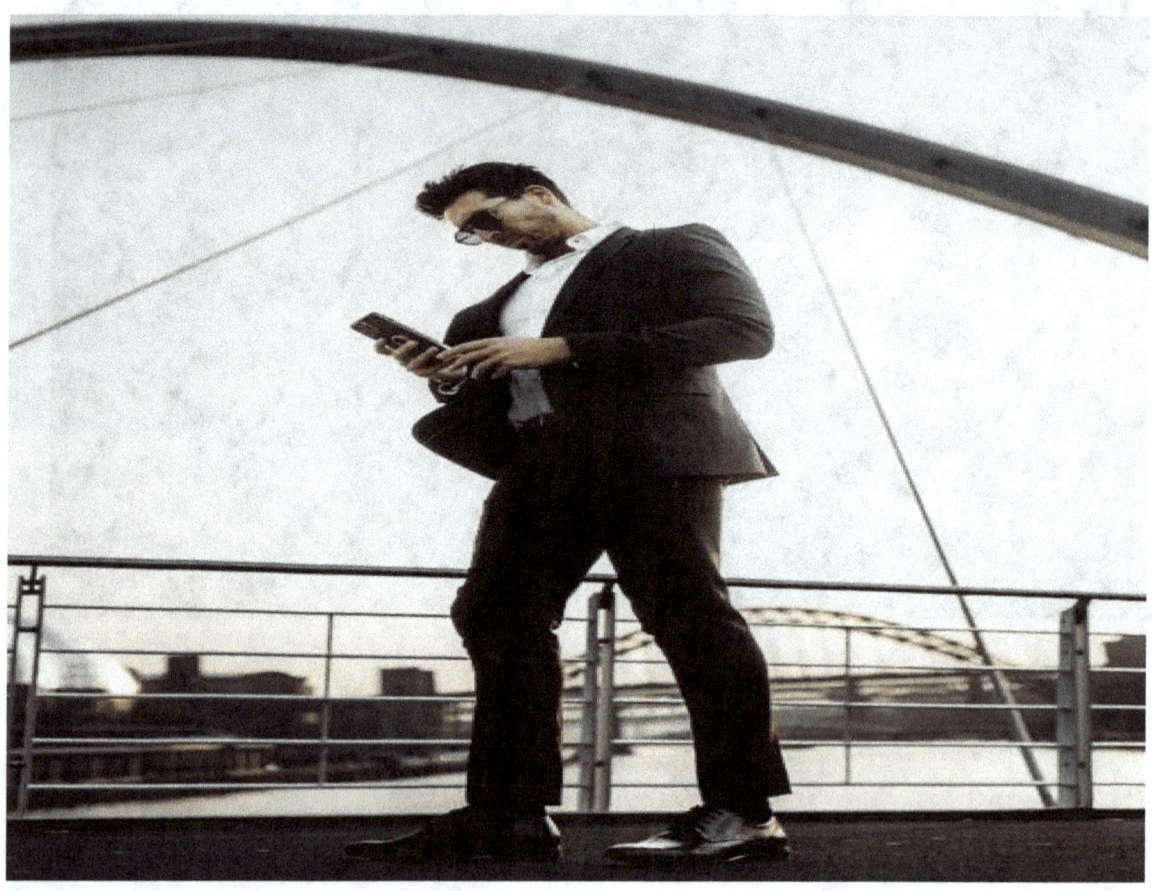

People are able to infer your wealth, level of organization, level of happiness, and level of sadness based on how you present yourself.

ACTING EXERCISES

Actors' Pre-Performance Stretches and Warm-Ups

As an actor, your performance on stage requires you to utilize your body's full capacity to succeed. An actor must be in touch with his instruments, just as a musician must be in touch with their instruments (his body). It would be best if you warmed your muscles before you go on stage so that people will take you seriously. Start with the things that are mentioned down below.

This exercise aims to relax your muscles and increase their range of motion by stretching each individual portion of your body. You will first separate your body into its component components to accomplish this.

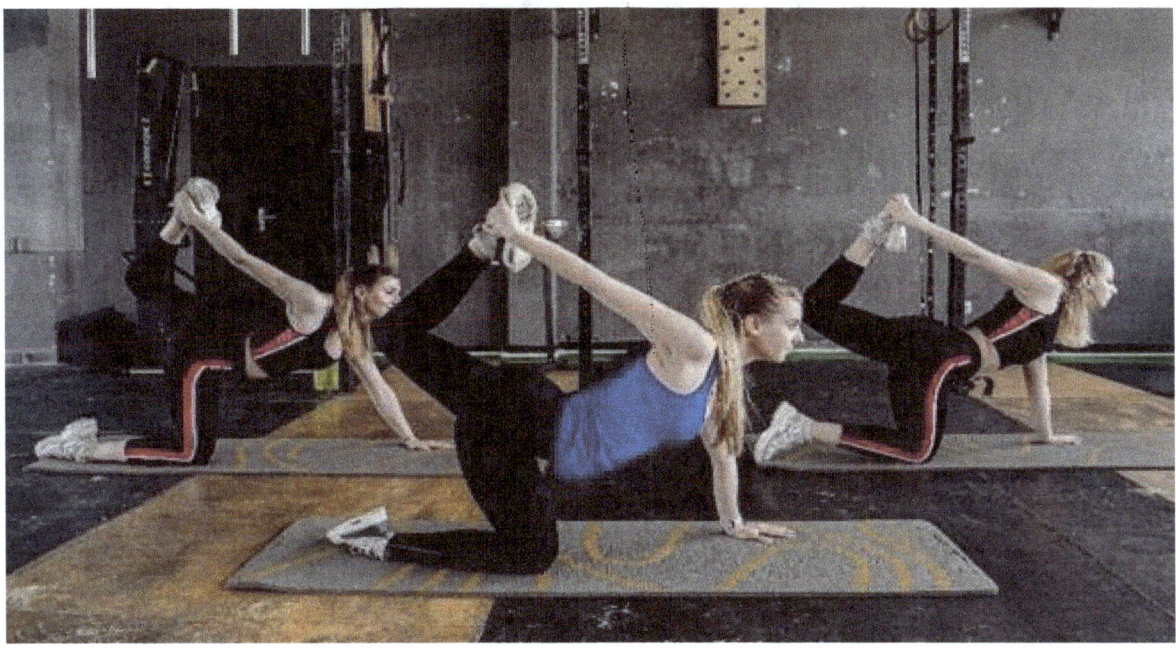

- Shaking is an effective method for relieving tension since it causes the body to shake.
- Stretching your face is the focus of this particular exercise, which is designed to lengthen and loosen the muscles in your face.

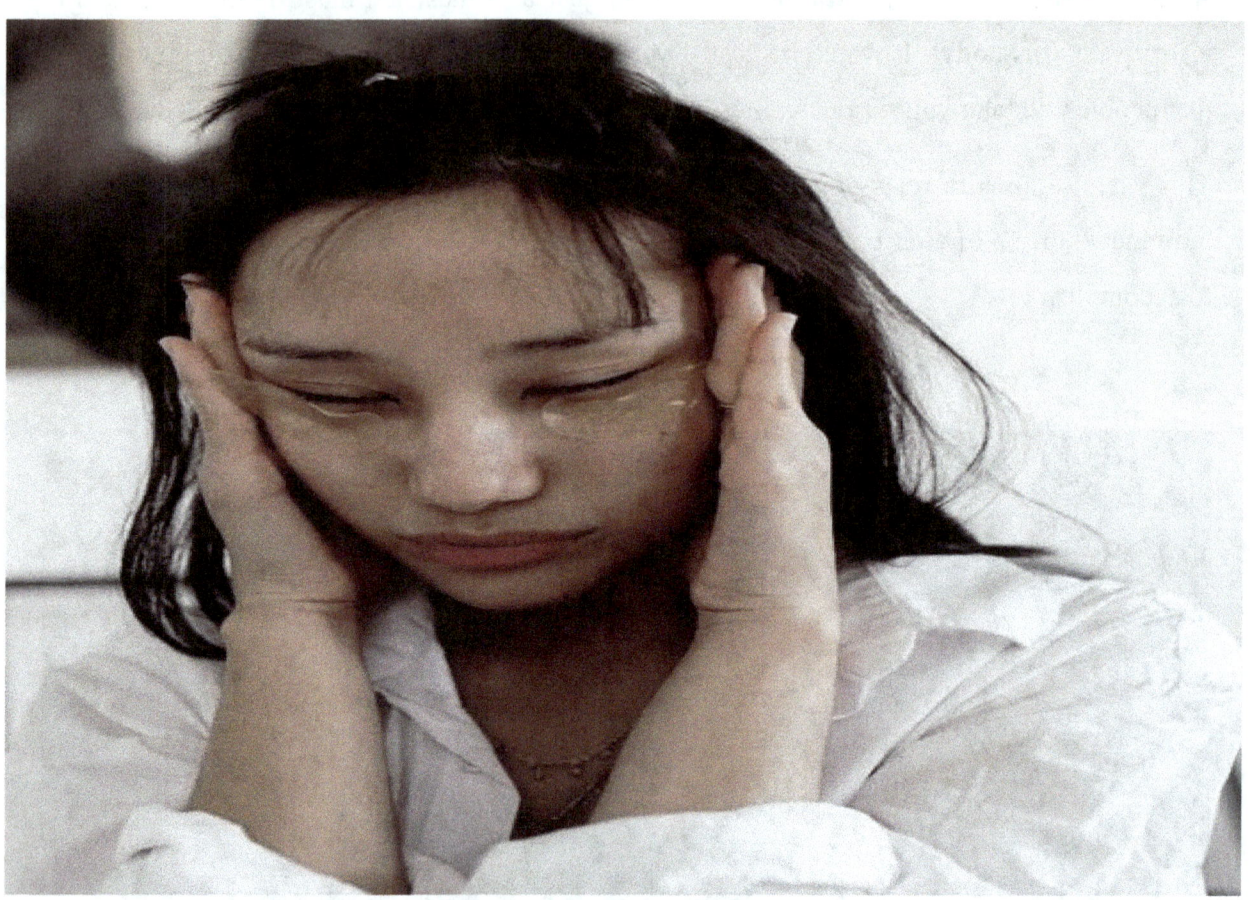

HOW TO PREPARE FOR ACTING

Nicely. Now, you have been summoned back and are expected to perform in the main event. You have previously auditioned for a play, and you have already done so. You may get ready by doing the following:

➢ **Memorize your lines**

As an actor, the very least you can do for your craft is to commit your lines to memory. If you do not commit your lines to memory, you will find that you frequently forget what it is that you are supposed to say.

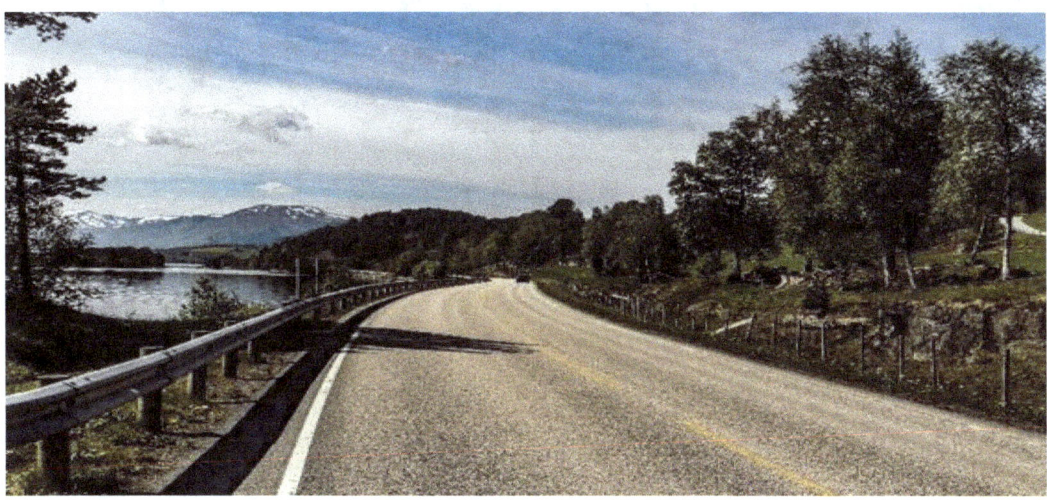

Do your homework

It is important that you are familiar with the setting of your scenarios. It is only through doing so that you will be able to comprehend the part that your character is intended to perform.

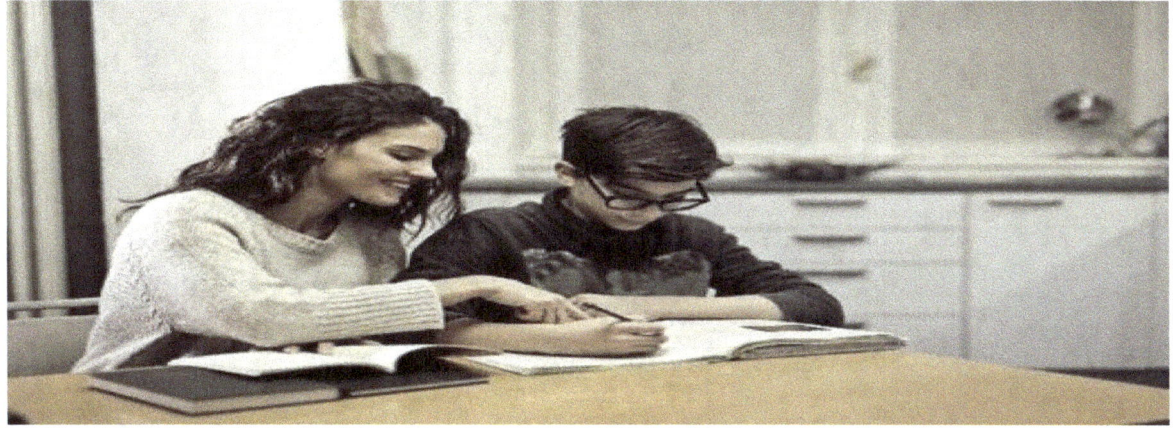

➢ **Rehearse**

You must devote a significant amount of time and effort into perfecting your role in an act before you can feel confident performing it for an audience. Practice it every day until you have a complete command of it.

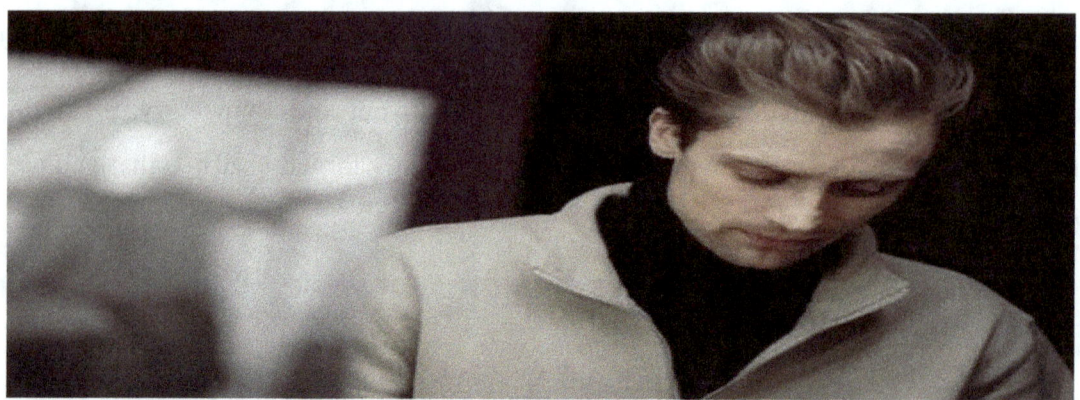

➢ **Rest**

Get a full night's sleep the night before the performance so that you can be at your best. You wouldn't want to go on stage feeling drowsy or weak. So, have some good slumber.

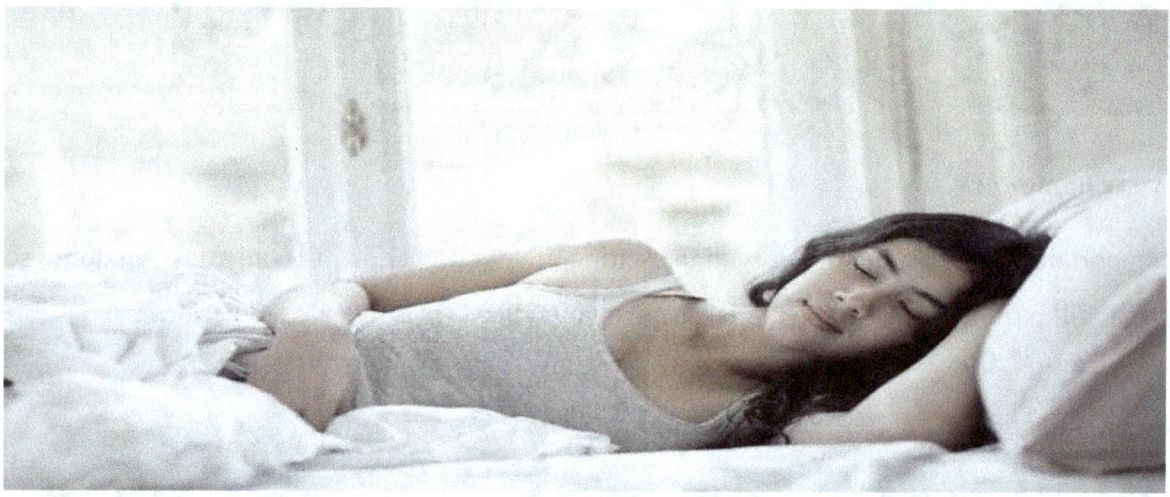

PART TWO: AUDITION

AUDITION

An act performed briefly before a casting director, or a panel of casting directors to be considered for a role in a play is called an audition. After watching an actor's performance, the casting director or the panel of casting directors must determine whether or not the actor is suitable to portray a certain character in the play.

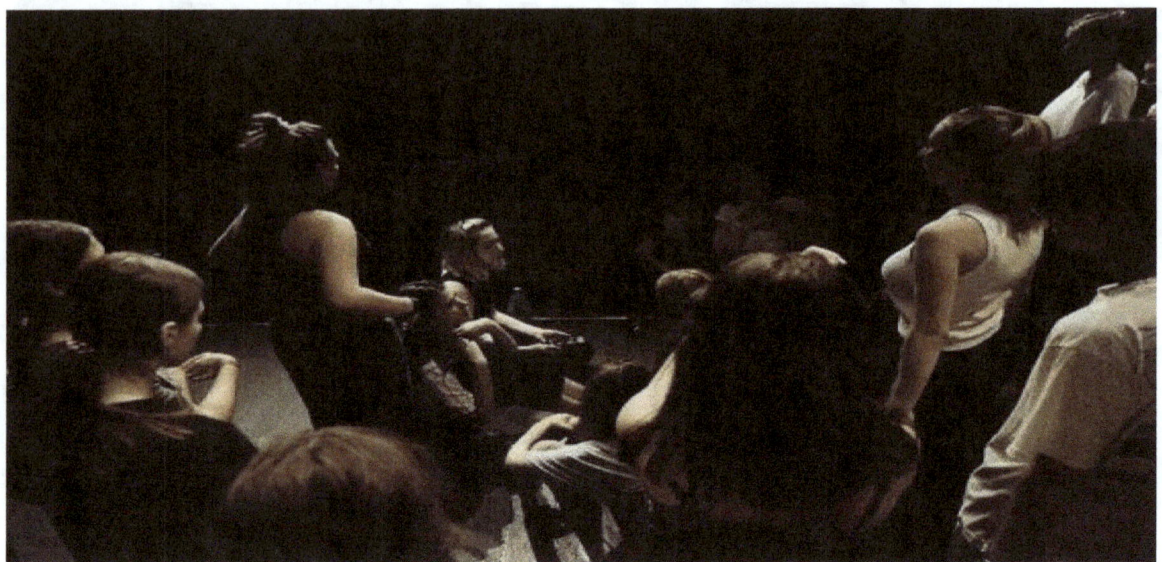

WHAT IS THE PURPOSE OF AN AUDITION?

The purpose of an audition is not to choose who will play a role but rather to determine who will be remembered. The audition aims to get the part, but the primary function of the audition is to wow the casting panel to the point that they want to see you again to consider you for future roles. In addition, if they remember your performance well, they could consider casting you in a position that requires acting.

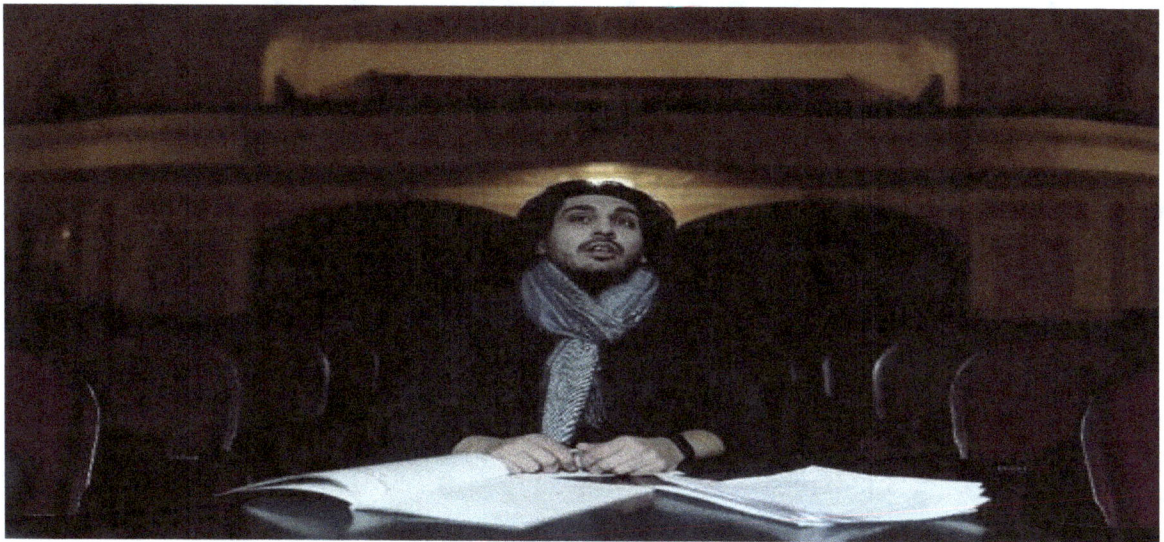

And if you want your audition to be remembered, you need to put in the effort to prepare effectively.

HOW TO PREPARE FOR AUDITION FOR A PLAY

✓ **Read the play!**

Before you can even begin to comprehend the deeper meaning behind the play in which you are going to have a role, you have to be familiar with the specifics of the scene in which you will be featured. Reading the play is an absolute need at this point.

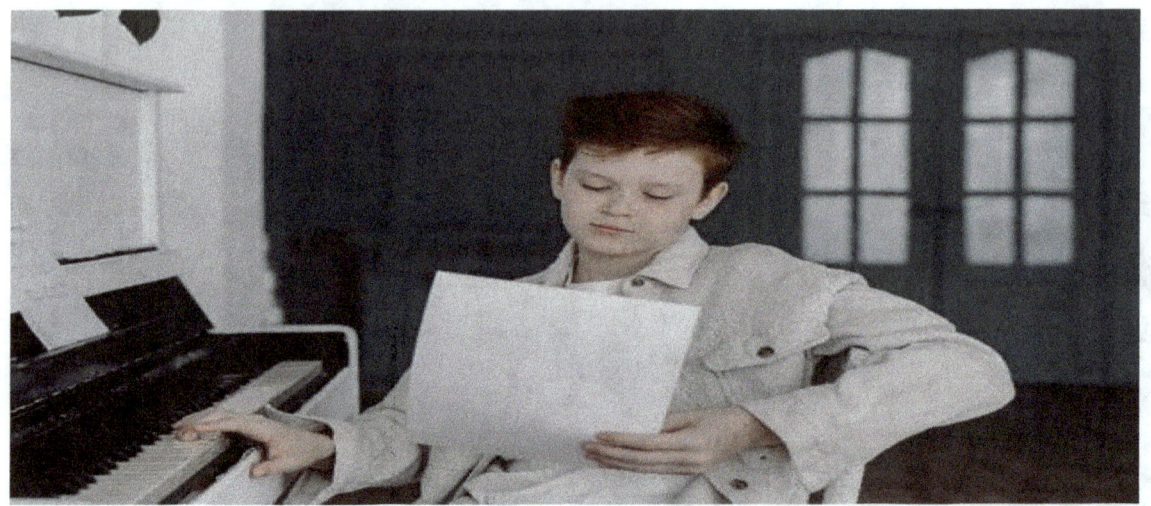

- ✓ **Read the play backward (not literally)**

If the last argument failed to inspire you, this one may. It will help if you read through the play as often as possible. Put your thoughts into the role you will play, and do as much research as possible on the person you are going to portray. The casting panel will ask you questions to determine how well you know about the role that you are expected to portray. If you understand your character well, you will be in a better position to answer these questions.

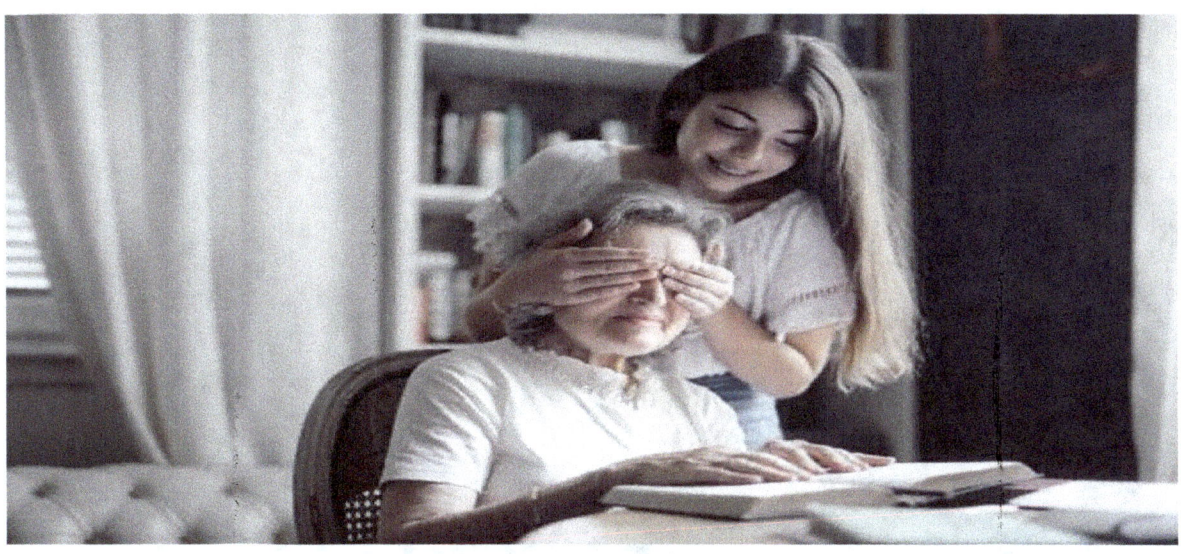

- ✓ **Practice your piece in several ways**

Use different ways to rehearse your piece. You can rehearse with your mother, father, siblings, or best friend. Instruct them to ask you to do the task in various ways, like the casting director.

✓ **Put on something that is both suitable and comfy.**

If you have the opportunity to audition for a role, you should dress in a manner that is consistent with the persona you intend to portray in the role. During your audition, you shouldn't be completely decked out in costume, but you should dress in a manner connected to the role you are trying out for. Dressing up in something more official and professional might be appropriate if, for instance, the part you are going to portray is that of a businessperson. You might ask your parents to choose an outfit for you that is appropriate for the occasion.

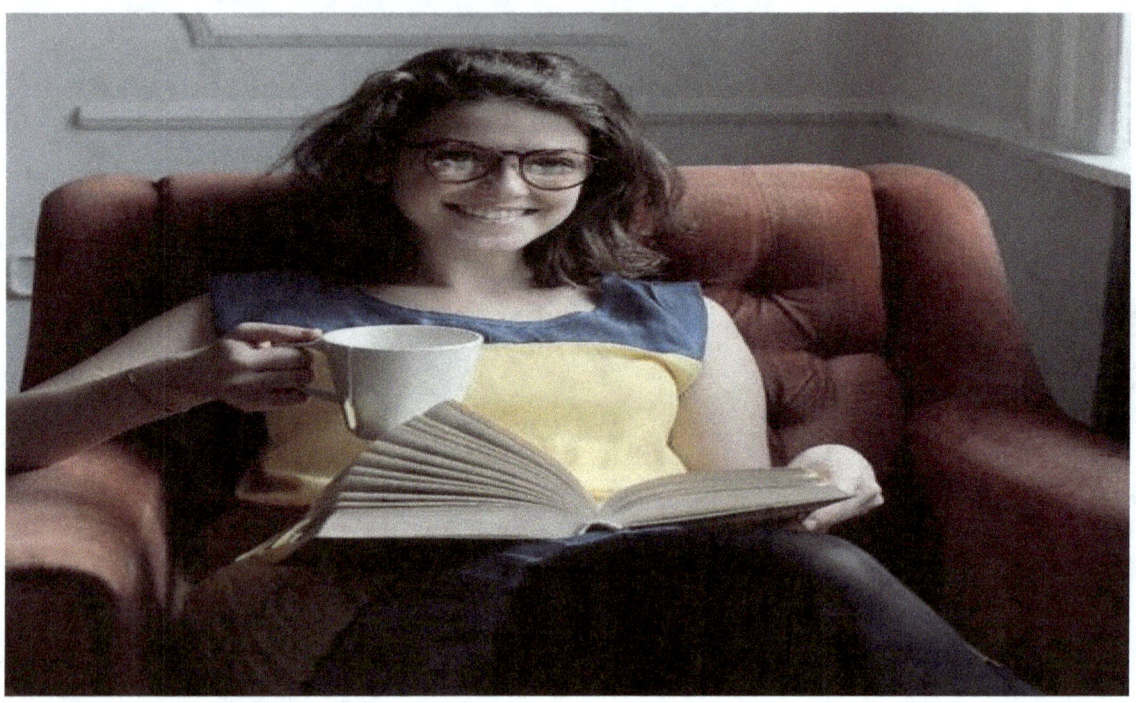

✓ **Warm up before auditioning**

The act of getting warm is significant. In addition to getting you physically ready, it also helps you hone your mental concentration.

✓ **Learn everything you can.**

Many people leave the audition room without making a good impression on the casting panel since they did not read the whole story beforehand. It is a horrible thing! Even though there isn't much information given to help you understand your character, you should still read everything and grasp the plot's setting. This is because, even though your primary focus should be on the part of the plot that involves your character, you should still understand the setting.

HOW TO ANALYZE THE PLAY

The most important job of an actor is to study a play to depict the characters honestly on stage. This requires them to discover the genuine essence of their character.

> **The first read**

When you first see the play, take your time and make sure you watch it all the way through. During this first reading, it is not necessary to pay close attention to the specific phrases or scenes; rather, you should just read the play from beginning to end to understand what the play is about.

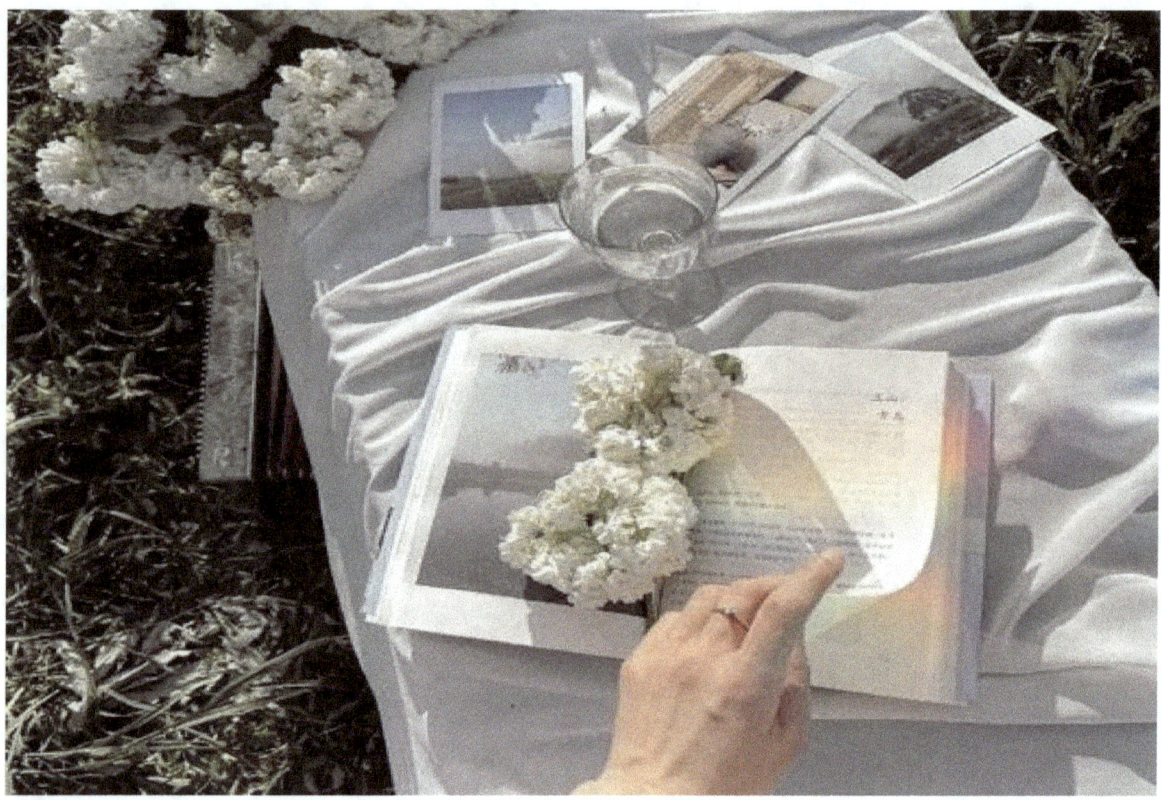

➤ A breakdown into scenes and beats

After you have finished reading everything, comprehended the character's function in the play, and obtained an overall understanding of what the play is about, you are ready to go on to the next step, developing a scene and beat map for the story. When it comes to a good play, scene A leads to scene B, which then leads to scene C, and so on. Your scenes need to be broken down into beats so that you can easily go from one character to another. This will allow you to be more fluid in your performance.

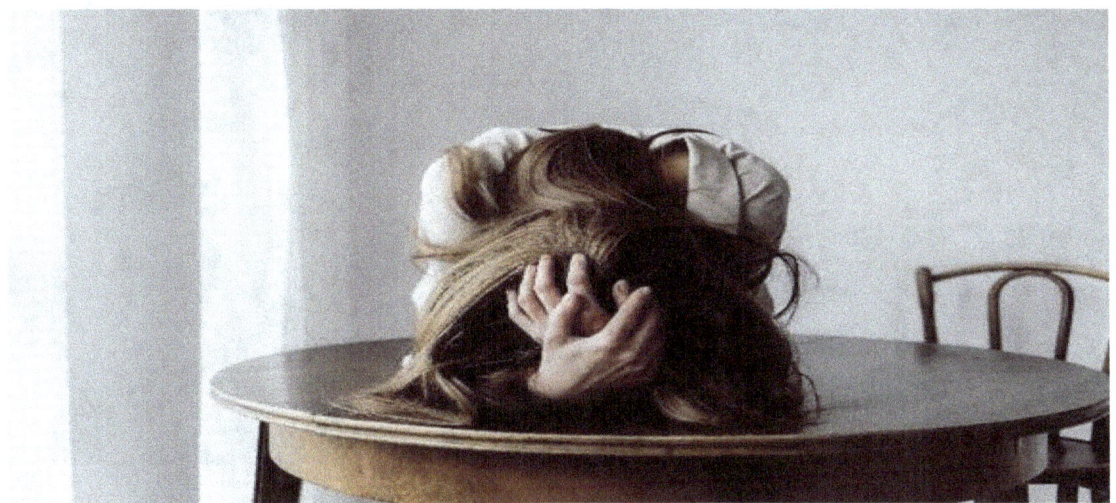

➤ Identify your characters' actions.

You will need to examine the play to figure out the acts that are appropriate for your character to take. Because you are familiar with all the acts, you are now aware of how to smoothly transition from one movement to the next without bewildering the audience.

> **Maintain an open mind to feedback and alterations.**

Bear in mind that for an act to be successful, the judges will provide feedback about the aspects of your performance that they enjoyed as well as those that they disliked. Please pay attention to what the director has to say in light of what they saw from your play, and then make the necessary adjustments.

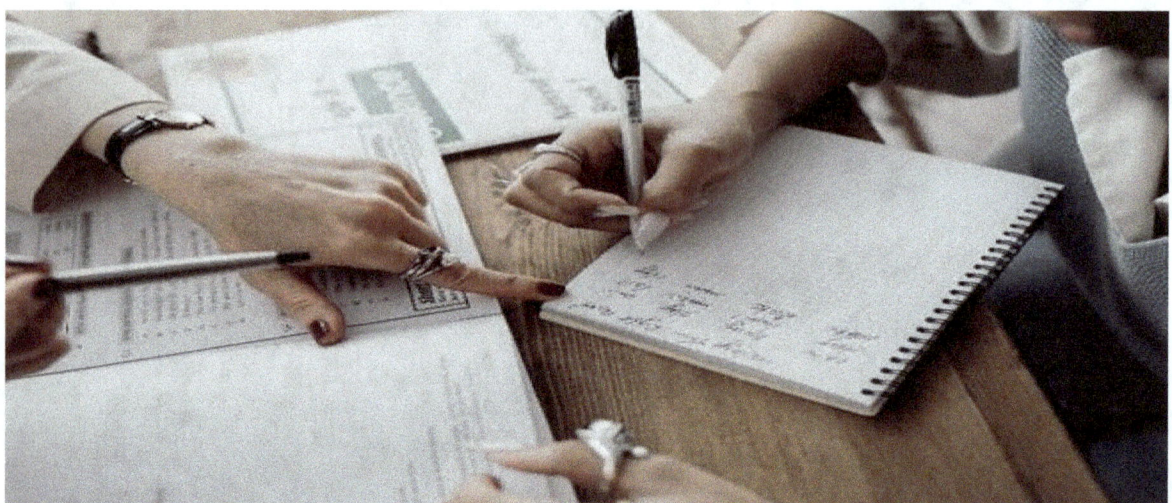

You may only capture part of the performance perfectly every time; hence, you must make a few adjustments as you progress through the rehearsal process. On the other hand, if you put everything described here into place, you will naturally and impressively perform exceptionally well.

How to Memorize Lines for a Play

If you have little time to memorize your lines before your audition, what steps would you take to ensure that your audition goes as smoothly as possible from the very beginning? When you have little time to practice for an audition, learning your lines by heart will help you do well. You can remember your lines more quickly if you use the strategies below.

✓ **Write your lines out.**

You will easily remember your lines if you write them down on paper first. Take notes as you go along with your practice.

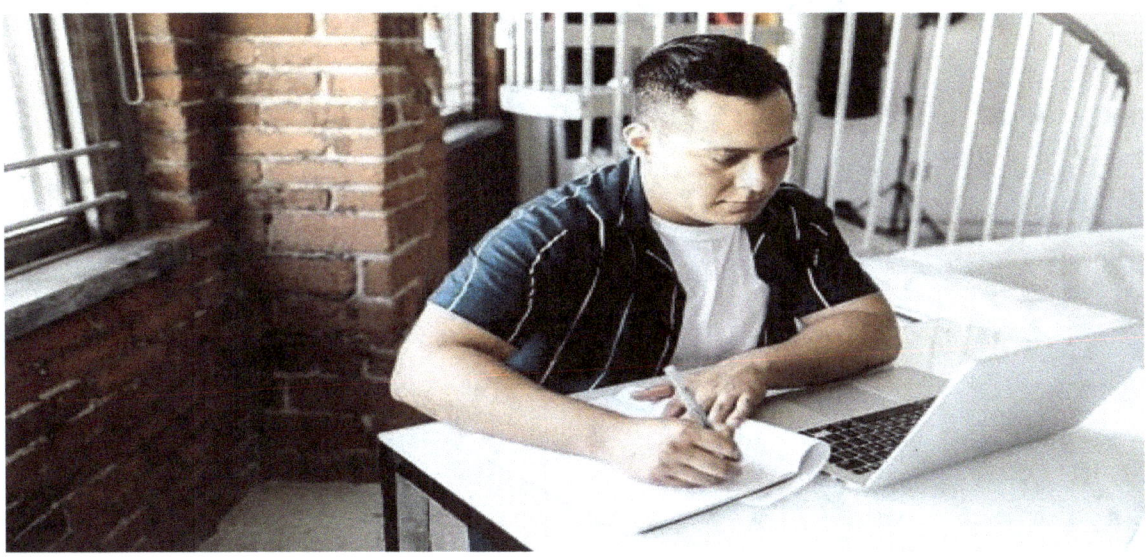

✓ **Run lines with someone**

Reciting a sentence aloud to someone else is one of the most effective memory techniques. You might consider running it with a fellow actor rather than a buddy from the neighborhood since they will be able to advise you more effectively.

- ✓ **Quiz yourself**

It would help if you gave this method a shot because many performers have found it useful for them. It is helpful to cover everything else with a sheet of paper except the sentence you are attempting to commit to memory. Repeatedly reading the passage, you are attempting to commit to memory is the best way to ensure that it will be retained. If you're having trouble getting through it, try reading it without looking at it.

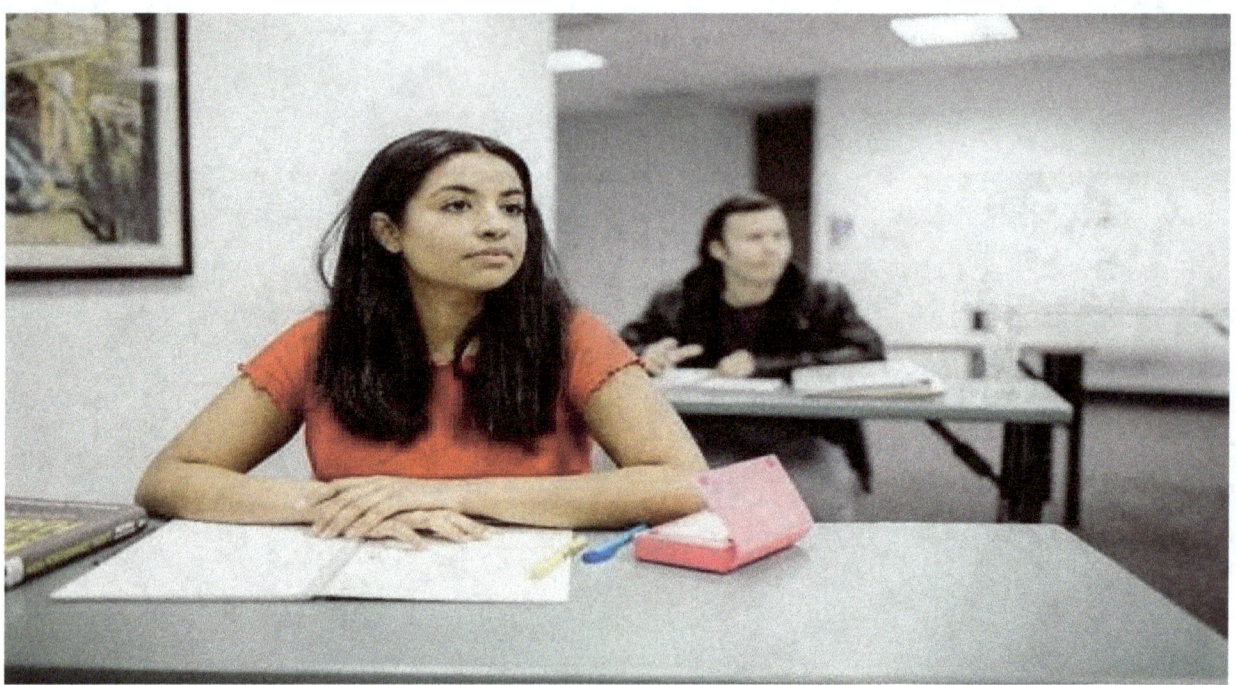

- ✓ **Take a nap**

Get some rest when you've hopefully mastered the material by then. In point of fact, when you are asleep, your brain moves the data that it has just finished processing from your short-term memory to your long-term recall, where it is stored in a format that is much easier for you to remember.

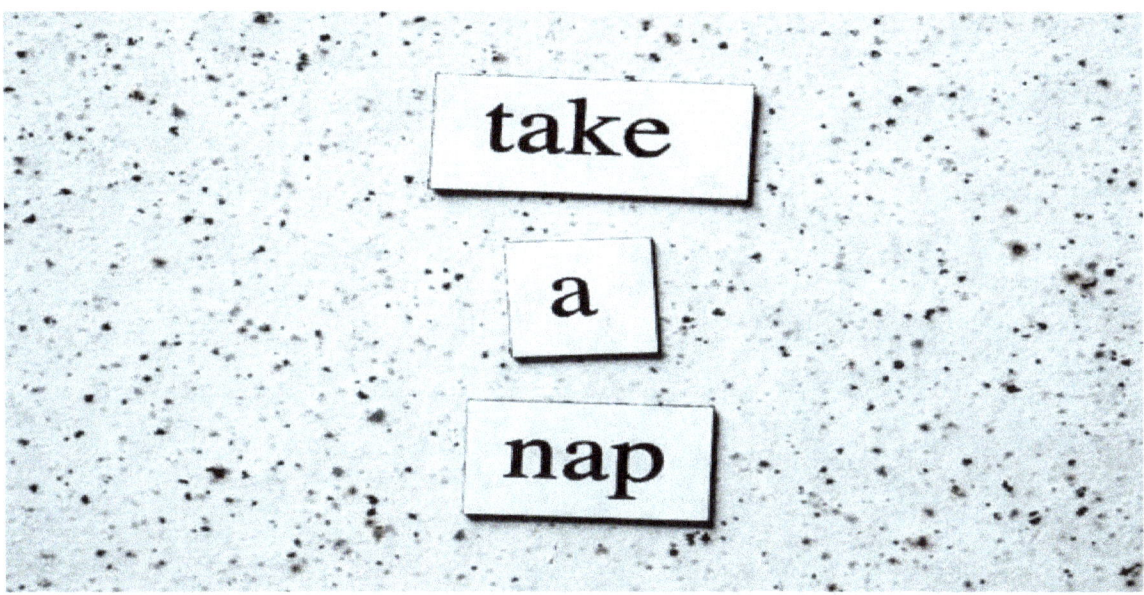

- ✓ **Use a mnemonic device.**

There is a way to remember a word or a string of words referred to as the "mnemonic method." In this approach, you recall the word or string of words by using the initial letter of each word in the string. Try outlining the initial letter of each word in your lines. After you have done that, continuing to look at those letters will make it much simpler for you to recall. Take a shortcut by employing this method.

- ✓ **Get familiar with the cue lines.**

Not only should you memorize your lines, but you should also master the cue lines, which are the lines that are said before your lines. If you are familiar with cue lines, you will be more punctual and be able to deliver your lines on time.

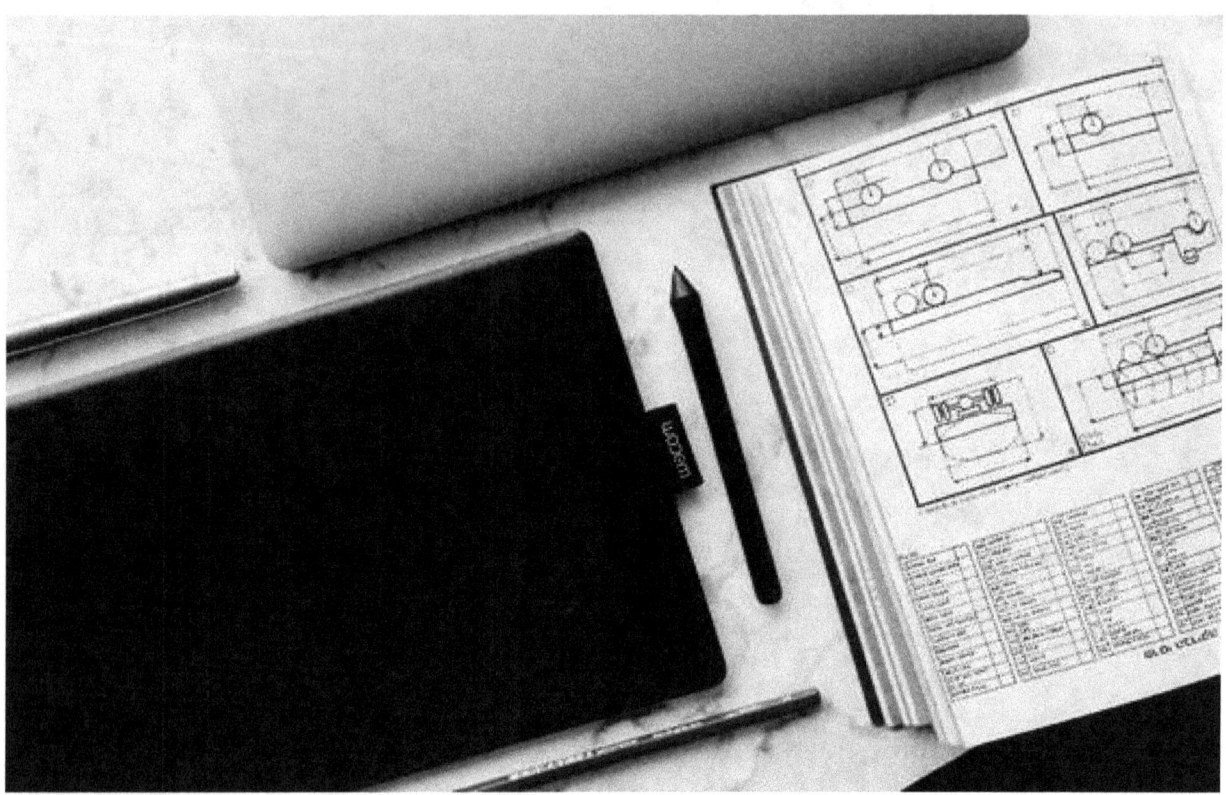

PART THREE: FINAL REHEARSAL WITH COSTUME— PRESENTATION WITH AUDIENCE

HOW TO GET THE AUDIENCE INVOLVED IN YOUR PRESENTATION

On stage, one of the most common errors that I see new performers make is failing to engage their audiences, which is a huge missed opportunity. I'm going to explain below two simple tactics that you can use to connect with and incorporate your audience in any presentation you're giving.

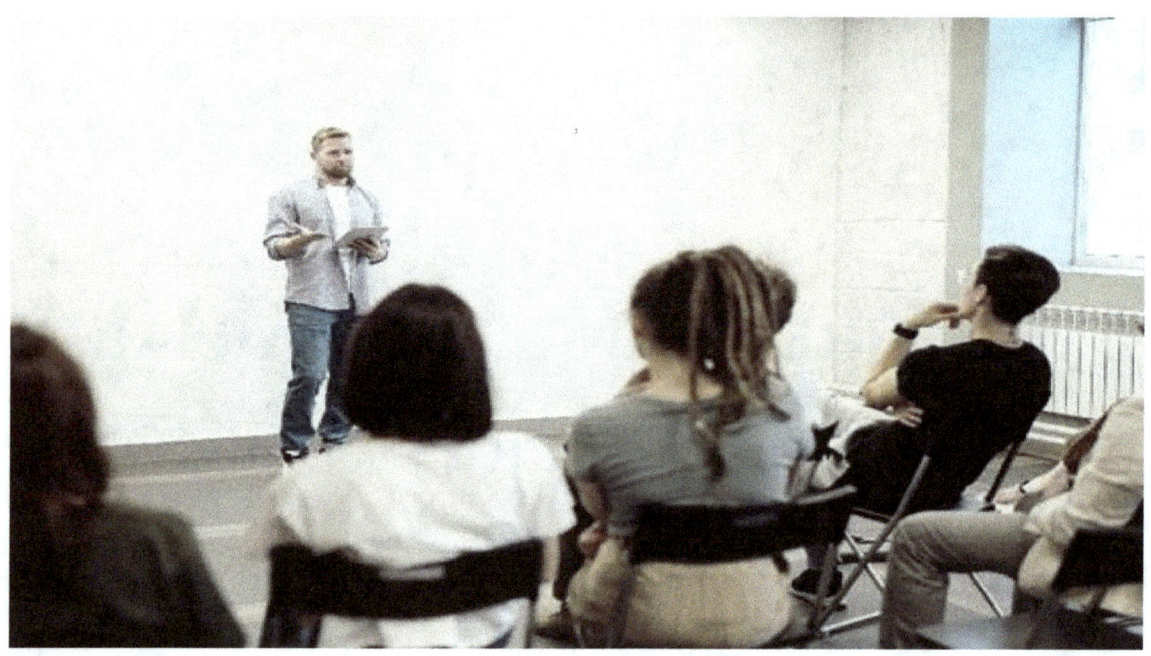

✓ Making eye contact

You must have observed that when individuals keep their eyes locked on you when you are talking to them, it gives you the impression that they are paying attention to what it is that you are saying. Do you suppose that you will be able to converse with them?

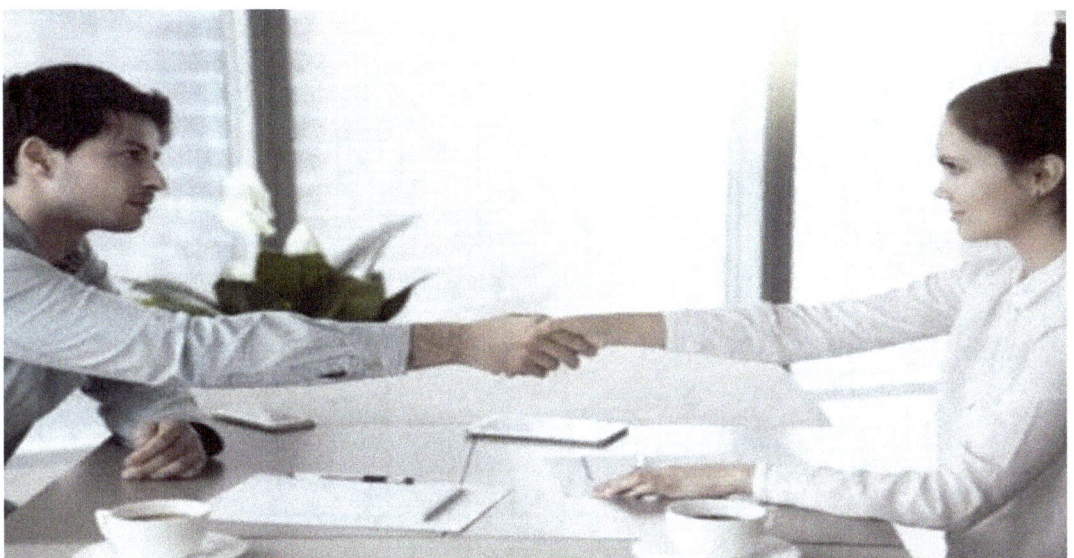

In a similar vein, it is essential to carry out such actions when performing. The excitement of the presentation is increased when the presenter is able to and is brave enough to maintain eye contact with the audience. Additionally, this energy will enable you to express who you are while simultaneously boosting your self-confidence. Simply said, it is an essential ability to possess.

✓ **Memorize your lines**

This topic has been brought up previously, and it will be discussed once again here since it is highly significant. Be certain that you have every line of your play thoroughly committed to memory and that you are able to deliver it in an excellent manner. You shouldn't be seen laboring to recall your line when you're performing on stage.

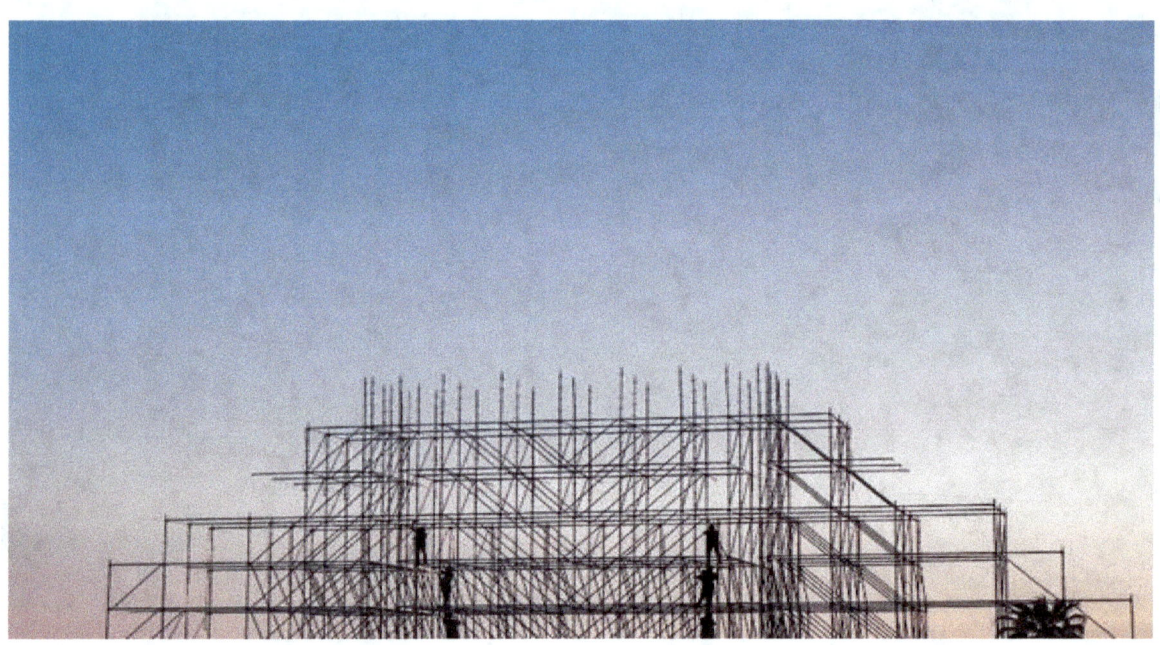

Ways for Effective Presentation

If you want your presentation to genuinely resonate with the audience, there are some presenting skills that you really need to have.

❖ **Maintain a Commanding Presence**

You need to have the ability to command the presence of the audience. You need to talk with tone and emotion, project your voice, walk with confidence, and be in control of your body posture.

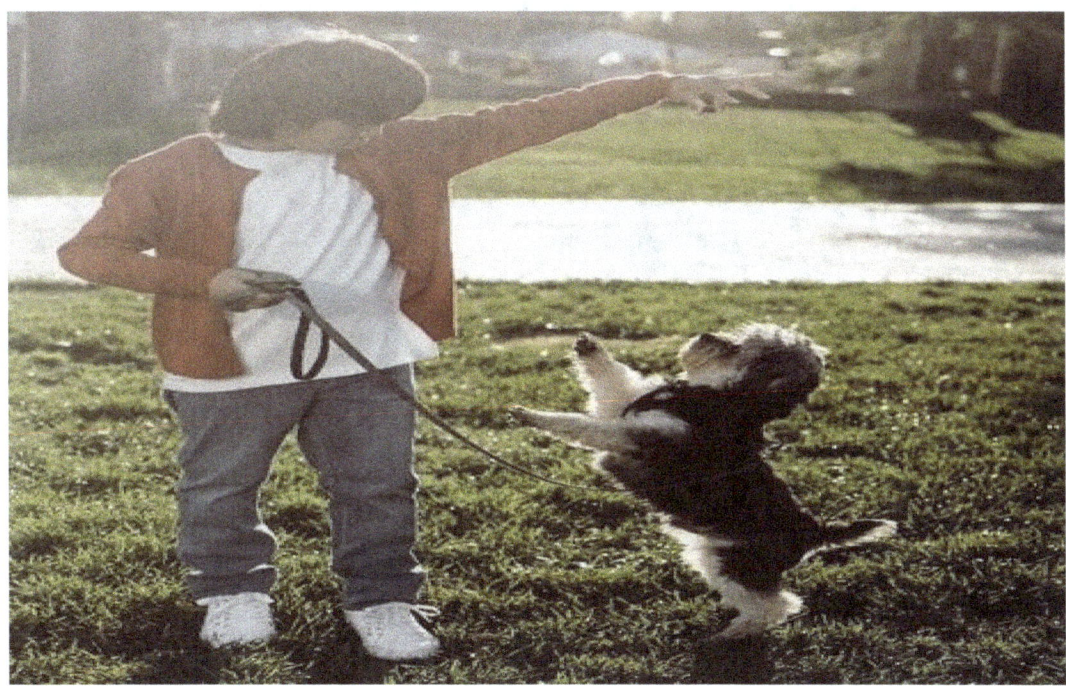

❖ **Know your content**

Before the day of the presentation, make sure you are comfortable with your piece. Before you can give a good performance of your line and gain the favor of the audience, you will need to study it well and rehearse it several times.

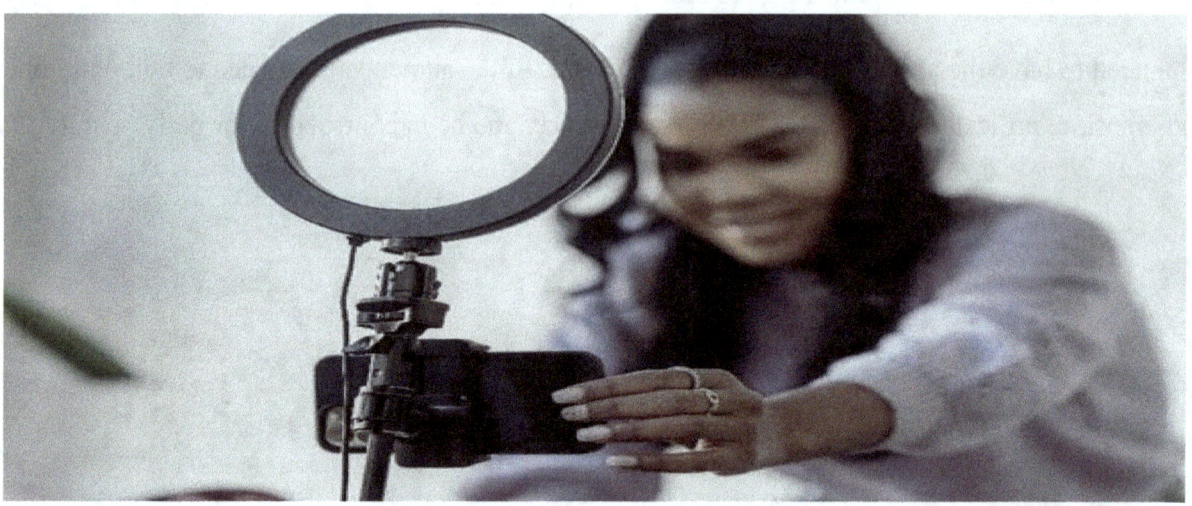

❖ **Find the light**

When performing on stage, actors must be continually aware of the direction from which the light is coming and avoid standing in regions that are too dark. If you are standing in a location that has low lighting, the audience will not be able to see you. It is your responsibility to ensure that the people in the audience can see you, regardless of whether or not you can see the audience members yourself. Employ some of these methods with your audience and see how they react to your acts as you do them.

Dos and Don'ts of Acting and Presentation

Actors routinely violate proper theatrical etiquette for no other reason than the fact that they are not aware of what is expected of them. From the dress rehearsals to the actual performance, this part of the course will take you through the many things that you should and should not do.

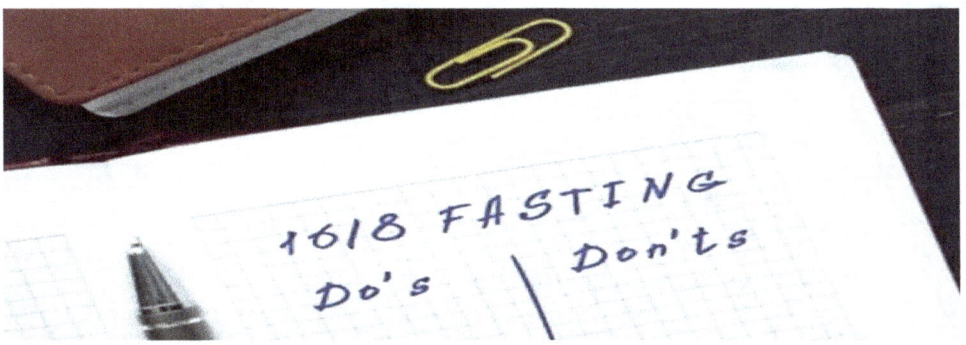

DO'S:

- Make sure that at some time throughout the performance you look directly into the eyes of each and every person in the audience. Even if it isn't always attainable, it is always helpful to the performer in connecting with the audience when it is accomplished.
- Remember your cues and lines at all times.
- Maintain a log of all of your movements, including coming in and going out of the building.
- Maintain your role for the entirety of your time on stage.
- It is important to be audible and clear when you are speaking on stage.
- Make sure that the people in the crowd can see your face. Always keep your back to them.

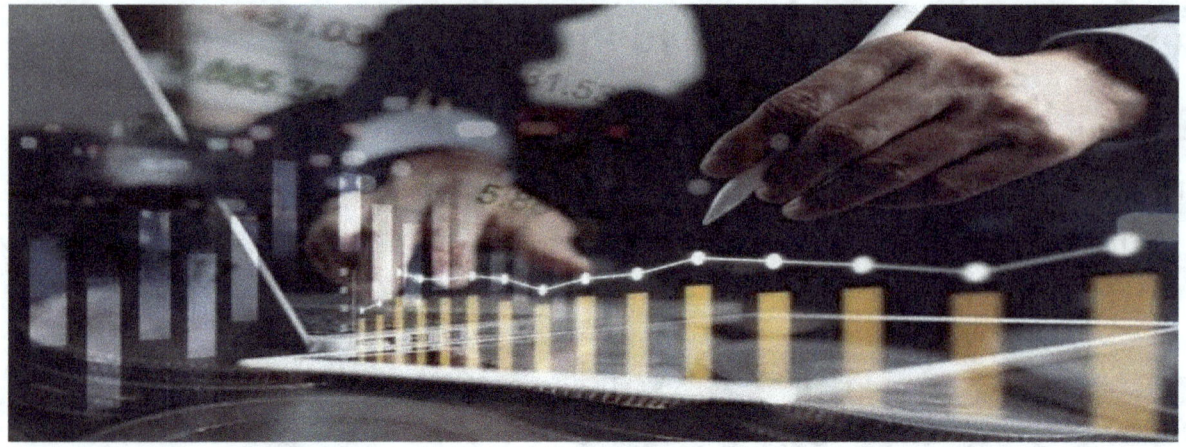

- At all times, be silent backstage.
- When you're done using your costume, make sure to store it properly.
- Take the play really seriously, and perform to the best of your ability.
- Be courteous to the other members of the cast, your fellow performers, the crew working backstage, and to yourself.
- As soon as you go onto the stage at the theater, give it everything you've got.
- Be a good member of the team.
- Have fun. The audience will notice if you are not having fun when you are performing, and they will understand that your heart is not truly in what you are doing.
- Keep a thankful attitude at all times. At the conclusion of the performance, you should express gratitude to the audience.

DON'TS

- You should avoid turning your back on the audience unless there is a specific point in the performance where it is essential to do so.
- It is important to refrain from touching other performers' personal things, including their costumes.
- During the performance, you shouldn't fiddle with your hair, props, or outfit.
- Onstage, you shouldn't be moving your feet at all.

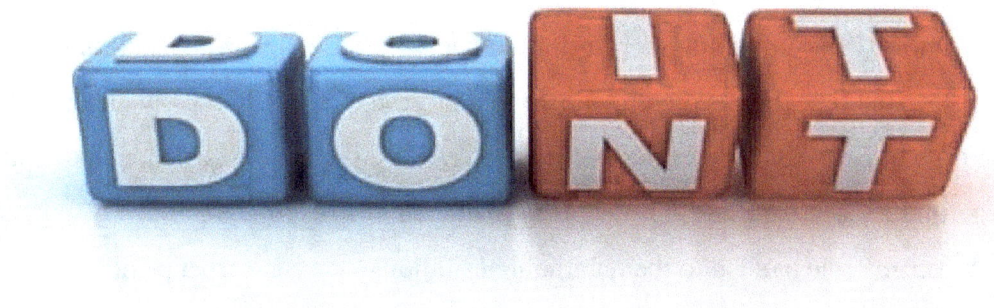

CONCLUSION

It would simplify things if you were born with a natural knack for acting. The ability to act is a talent. As is the case with every other talent, it is frequent. To become a good actor, however, it is not sufficient to have acting talent; to become a good actor, you must practice and refine your acting technique. And I hope that during this course, I have presented you with some fundamental knowledge about acting and tactics that you can use to strengthen your acting talents and perform with self-assurance while still being successful.

You now have tools at your disposal that will assist you in developing your acting talents, regardless of how excellent or poor they are. To enhance your skill, all that is asked of you is attention and effort. Please pay attention to how other actors do their roles and take cues from them, and at the same time, be devoted to doing what has to be done effectively. Those who have invested the time to become more proficient in their craft are the ones who are included in plays. They keep getting chosen for plays because they exude an air of self-assurance on stage and are willing to take on any role handed to them without hesitation. You can earn a position on the stage if you have the self-assurance and a willingness to participate in the game.

However, it is important to remember that only some of the performers whose work you like become experts overnight. They committed significant time and effort to hone their acting abilities. If you put in as much practice as possible, you'll improve your acting skills in no time.

ASSESSMENTS

EXERCISE 1

Student Will Interpret Different Animals

- Body Warm Up
- The instructor will have each student select an animal using a ballot that is kept hidden from them.
- The student will take on the role of a specific animal
- The remaining students are tasked with identifying the animal.
- Other students will appear on stage to do an animal interpretation.
- Every student must remain in their assigned place until the bell rings at 6.
- They will take on the roles of different animals.

EXERCISE 2

Student will interpret different emotions (sad, happy, worried, tired, cheerful, Furious etc.,)

- Body Warm Up
- The instructor will lead the class in selecting an emotion from a ballot that is kept hidden.
- The student will speak his or her name while expressing the selected feeling (individual) TEACHER WILL guide TO DIFERENTS EMOTION

EXERCISE 3

Grin Or Smirk

- Students will be called up to the stage by the instructor. They are going to stand face to face in order to grin and sneer at each other.

EXERCISE 4

Sadness

- The students will be brought up to the stage one at a time. They are required to pick an actual life circumstance. A tragic turning point in their lives.

EXERCISE 5

Happiness

- The student will be called in by the teacher to discuss a positive episode in her or his life.

EXERCISE 6

Monologue

- A student will be selected to read a monologue that the teacher has chosen. The identical speech will be read aloud by each student.

EXERCISE 7

Dialogue

- 2 pupils on stage. They will engage in role play to learn how to hold conversations.
- The instructor will pay attention to the students' diction, voice volume, posture, and eye contact.

EXERCISE 8

Environment

- On stage, the instructor will direct the kids to work on issues pertaining to the environment, the weather, and their ages.

EXERCISE 9

Various Industry Categories or Types of Working Positions

- The instructor will direct the kids through the process of doing a variety of adult professions and vocations.
- The students will be required to improvise. They will make use of props if they are available.

EXERCISE 10

Action scenes, sometimes known as the physical scene

- The instructor will direct the class in the performance of a variety of various kinds of scenarios. The instructor directs the pupils in various activities such as a fight or dance scenario, etc.

EXERCISE 11

Helping Others

- On stage, the instructor will put the students in a variety of scenarios to test how they respond to different challenges, such as having one of their classmates become ill.

EXERCISE 12

911 Call

- The student is expected to improvise. The instructor will assemble pupils on the stage to take care of the 911 call.
- As an illustration, grandma gets sick and collapses in the middle of the stage. The teacher will have some of the other pupils help.

EXERCISE 13

Different Type of Voices

> The instructor will direct the student to imitate several sorts of voices, such as a child's voice, an adult's voice, a low voice, and a loud voice.

EXERCISE 14

Play With an Object

> The instructor will invite each student individually to the center of the stage so that they can choose an imagined bird, butterfly, or other creature. They will recite a line during the performance.

EXERCISE 15

Performance a Character

> Students will act out a variety of roles during the presentation. For instance, a guy or woman who is intoxicated, a sick child, etc.

EXERCISE 16

Description

> The instructor is going to bring a student up to the front of the class. The remainder of the essay will focus on the individual student. (The student is white, has black hair, eyes that are hazel, is tall and powerful, and has a slender build.)

EXERCISE 17

Frustration

- The teacher called a few students to the front of the room. The teacher would then send a student to ask for help in a language that they cannot understand.

EXERCISE 18

Pain

- When the teacher calls a student to the stage, the student pretends to trip. He is hurting. The teacher makes other students help. They need to make do. (The teacher will show the students the way. The teacher will make sure they don't cover their faces, change their voices or words, turn away from the audience, etc.

EXERCISE 19

Trapped Calling for Help

- Send a student to the stage, said the teacher. He or she will act like they're stuck somewhere. The student will get help. (The teacher will show the student how to bring out different feelings, like panic, fear, desperation, etc.)

EXERCISE 20

THE USE OF THE PROMPTER

- Teacher calls student to the front of the room. The student's teacher will tell them what to say. The teacher will help the student get the right feelings.

GRADUATION

Final Step

> Each student will present a 3 to 5 minutes monologue. This presentation could be in front a live audience or a video recorded.

INSTRUCTOR SUBJECT THE FOLLOWING TOPICS.

1. 5 THINGS OR WAYS YOU SHOULD DO TO BE A GOOD CITIZEN
2. 5 WAYS YOU SHOULD DO TO SHOW GRATITUDE
3. 5 WAYS YOU SHOULD DO TO SHOW INTEGRITY
4. 5 WAYS YOU SHOULD DO TO SHOW PATIENCE
5. 5 WAYS YOU SHOULD DO TO SHOW COOPERATIVE
6. 5 WAYS YOU SHOULD DO TO SHOW KIND OR KINDNESS
7. 5 WAYS YOU SHOULD DO TO SHOW RESPECTFULL
8. 5 WAYS YOU SHOULD DO TO SHOW RESILIENCE
9. 5 WAYS YOU SHOULD DO TO SHOW RESPONSIBLE
10. 5 WAYS YOU SHOULD DO TO SHOW PERSEVERANCE
11. 5 WAYS YOU SHOULD DO TO SHOW FAIR OR FAIRNESS
12. 5 THINGS YOU SHOULD DO TO BE A SUPERHERO

GLOSSARY

Act - perform a role in a play, film, or television

Acting - the art or occupation of performing fictional roles in plays, films, or television

Action - used by a film director as a command to begin

Actor - a participant in an action or process

Actress - a woman whose profession is acting on stage, in films, or on television

Attention - the action of dealing with or taking special care of someone or something

Audience - the people who watch or listen to a television or radio program

Audition - an interview for a role or job, consisting of a practical demonstration of the candidate's suitability and skill

Background - the part of a scene that forms a setting for the main figures or objects, or appears furthest from the viewer

Backstage - the area behind the stage in a theatre, especially the wings or dressing rooms

Break a leg - Theatrical Slang; Good Luck!

Beats - A momentary pause or delay in which there is a subtle shift in mood, thought, or feeling

Cues - a thing said or done that serves as a signal to an actor or other performer to enter or begin their speech or performance

Casting - to choose actors to play particular parts in a play, movie, or show

Comedy - a performance where there is a happy ending, with the intention of amusing and entertaining the audience

Casting director - the person responsible for assigning roles in a film or play

Credit - play at the beginning and end of nearly every film

Call back - an invitation to the actor, from the director of a show, to take the next step down the audition path

Description - a spoken or written account of a person, or event

Dialogue - conversations between characters

Diction - the style of enunciation in speaking of a character within the play

Director - a person who is responsible for the overall artistic vision of a production

Dressing up - to wear clothes of a certain kind or style

Drama - a play for theatre, or television

Character - a person portrayed in a scripted or devised play, novel, or another artistic piece

Characterization - How an actor uses body, voice, and thought to develop and portray a character

Communication - the exchanging of information by speaking, writing, or using some other medium

Conversation - a talk, especially an informal one, between two or more people, in which ideas are exchanged

Costume - a set of clothes worn by an actor or performer for a particular role

Cue Lines - the trigger for an action to be carried out at a specific time

Curtain - a screen of heavy cloth or other material that can be raised or lowered at the front of a stage

Gestures - any movement of the actor's body that is used to convey meaning, attitude, or feeling

Happiness - the state of being happy

Interpretation - the action of explaining the meaning of something

Imagination - a style of play that takes place in the mind rather than in the real world

Light - to draw focus to the character or element it is highlighting

Live audience - The audience at a play is the group of people watching or listening to it

Extra - a performer who appears in a nonspeaking (silent) capacity, usually in the background

Eye contact - nonverbal communication that humans use to communicate many forms of emotions

Eye gazing - the act of looking into someone's eyes for an extended amount of time

Emotion - represent reactions to other actors/characters' behavior and /or actions

Entertainment - the action of providing or being provided with amusement

Find the light - if you're in the dark on stage, step into the light source so you can be seen

Fear - an unpleasant emotion caused by the threat of danger, pain, or harm

Reading - the process of looking at a series of written symbols and getting meaning from them

Rehearsal – a session when actors are called to work through some scenes from the play in private

Romantic comedy - a film or play that deals with love in a light, humorous way

Run lines - memorizing lines; focus on simply running through the lines with another actor

Role - an actor's part in a play, film

Scene - a subdivision of a play

Script - the text of a play, also contains stage directions and other notes

Memorize - Committing something to memory; learn by heart

Mnemonic device - learning technique that aids information retention in the human memory for better understanding

Monologue - long speech made by one actor

Movement - refers to the action of the play as it moves from event to event

Movie – a cinema film

Non-verbal - not involving or using words or speech

Outfit - a set of clothes worn together, especially for a particular occasion or purpose

Outstanding - exceptionally good.

Personal - belonging to a particular person rather than anyone else

Play - represent (a character) in a theatrical performance or a film

Presentation - the giving of something to someone, especially as part of a formal ceremony

Prompter - a person offstage who reminds the actors of forgotten lines or cues.

Portrait - a dramatic representation of a character

Playwright – a person who creates plays

Performance - an act of presenting a play, concert, or other forms of entertainment

Practice - to perform or work over and over so as to become skilled

Space - describes where a drama is performed and how the actors use the space.

Speech - a sequence of lines written for one character in a play

Stage - the part of the theatre in which performances happen

Setting - when and where the action of a play takes place

Theatre - the physical building where plays are performed

Theatrical - exaggerated and excessively dramatic

Thespis – the first known individual to ever perform on stage

Tears – sorrow or crying

Television - a system for converting visual images (with sound) into electrical signals

Under five - a television or film actor whose character has fewer than five lines of dialogue

Vocal tone - the way a voice actor speaks

Voice - the combination of vocal qualities an actor uses

Warm up - prepares the actor's body for the performance by exercising

Writer – a person who writes plays, or dramas

Your body – body language of an actor

Perform - to entertain an audience by playing a piece of music, acting in a play

SABAT BEATTO

Books by Sabat Beatto

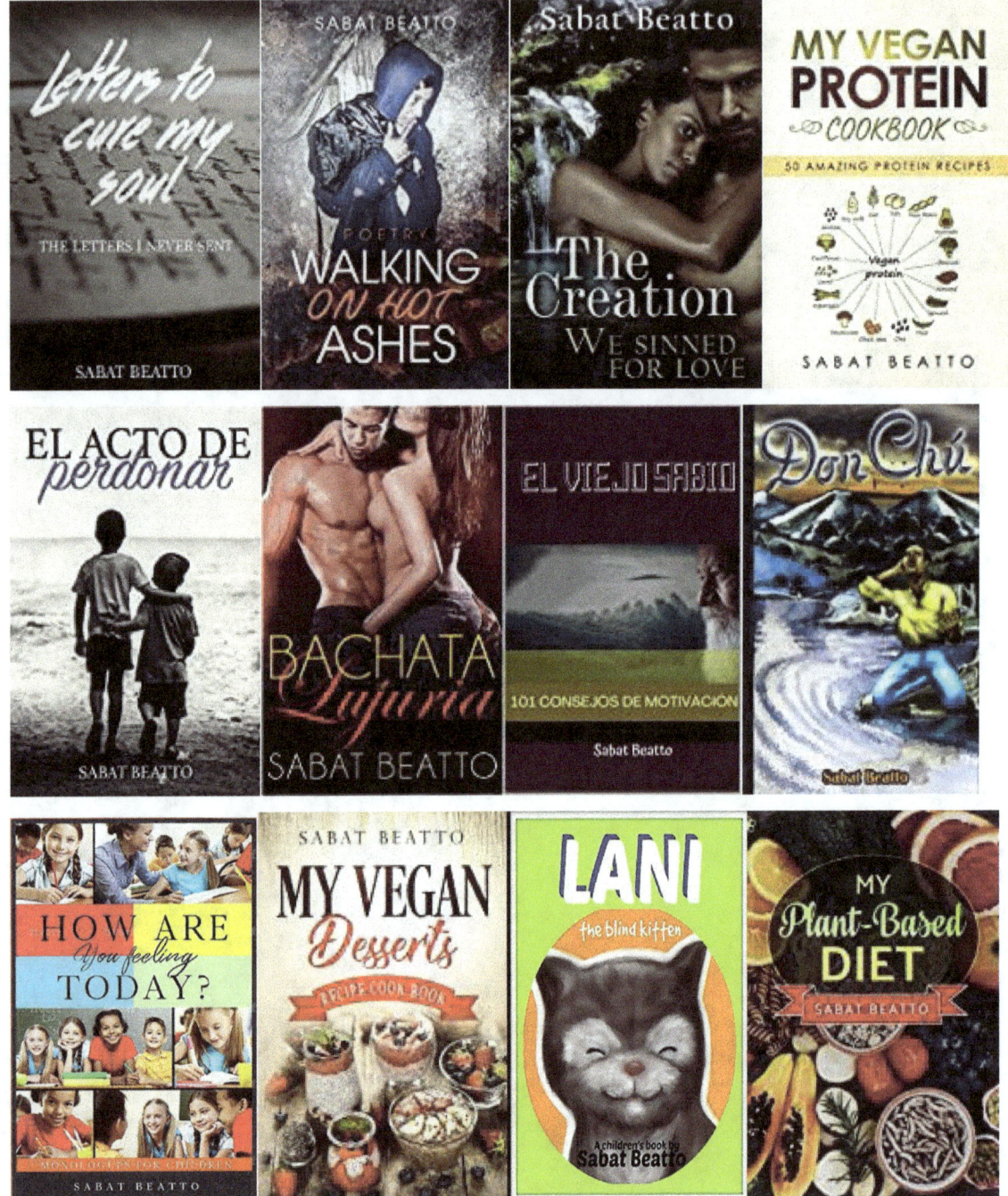

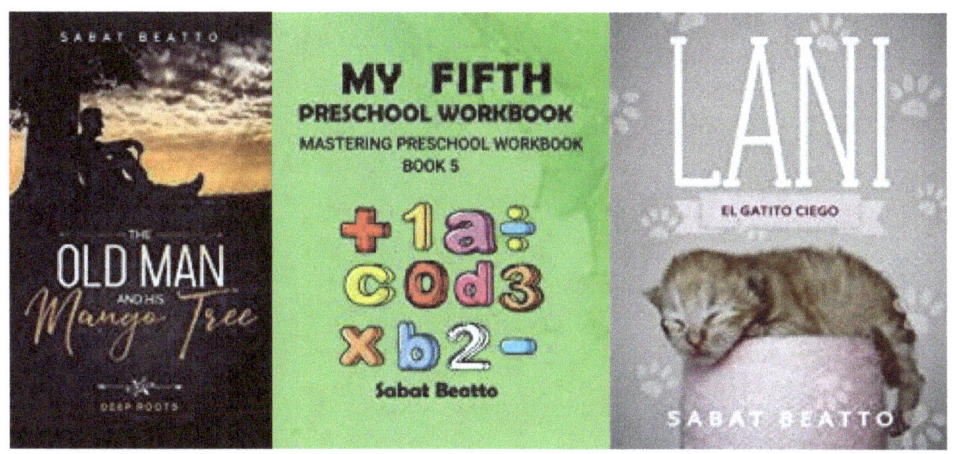
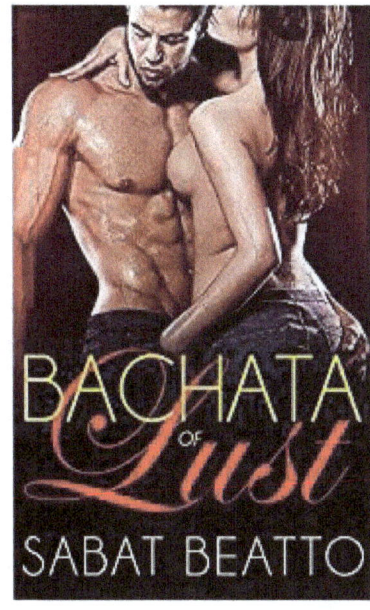
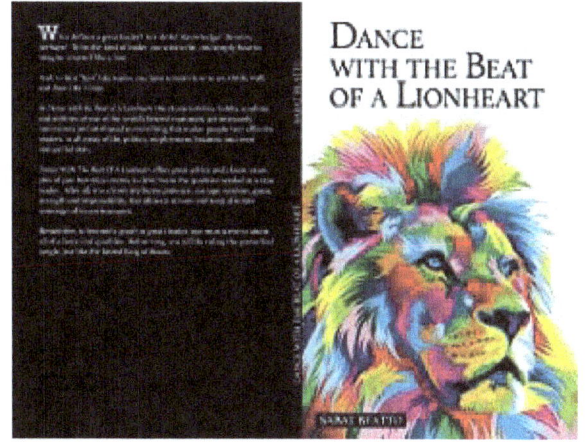

SABAT BEATTO

SABAT BEATTO

SABAT BEATTO

SABAT BEATTO

www.ingramcontent.com/pod-product-compliance
Lightning Source LLC
Chambersburg PA
CBHW060433220526
45465CB00008B/3128

www.ingramcontent.com/pod-product-compliance
Lightning Source LLC
Chambersburg PA
CBHW060433220526
45465CB00008B/3128